Sports in America

1960–1969

SECOND EDITION

DAVID FISCHER

SERIES FOREWORD BY
LARRY KEITH

CHELSEA HOUSE
PUBLISHERS
An imprint of Infobase Publishing

1960–1969, Second Edition
Sports in America

Chelsea House
An imprint of Infobase Publishing
132 West 31st Street
New York NY 10001

Library of Congress Cataloging-in-Publication Data

Fischer, David, 1963-
  Sports in America, 1960-1969 / David Fischer. — 2nd ed.
     p. cm.
  Includes bibliographical references and index.
  ISBN-13: 978-1-60413-453-7 (hardcover : alk. paper)
  ISBN-10: 1-60413-453-4 (hardcover : alk. paper)
  I. Title.

  GV583.F565 2010
  796.097309046—dc22

                    2009043274

Produced by the Shoreline Publishing Group LLC
President/Editorial Director: James Buckley Jr.
Contributing Editors: Jim Gigliotti, Beth Adelman
Text design and composition by Thomas Carling, carlingdesign.com
Index by Nanette Cardon, IRIS

Interior Photo Credits: AP/Wide World: 7, 12, 15, 17, 19, 22, 25, 27, 29, 34, 36, 39, 43, 44, 48, 53, 58, 63, 69, 71, 80, 81, 83, 85, 89; Corbis: 9, 10, 35, 47, 56, 65, 72, 75, 87; Getty Images: 3, 20, 28, 31, 52, 55, 59, 67, 76.
Sports icons by Bob Eckstein.

Cover printed by Bang Printing, Brainerd, MN
Book printed and bound by Bang Printing, Brainerd, MN
Date printed: July 2010
Printed in the United States of America.

10 9 8 7 6 5 4 3 2 1

CONTENTS

Olympic figure skating champion Peggy Fleming (page 76).

FOREWORD

BY LARRY KEITH

WHEN THE EDITORS OF SPORTS IN AMERICA invited me to write the foreword to this important historical series I recalled my experience in the 1980s as the adjunct professor for a new sports journalism course in the graduate school of Columbia University. Before granting their approval, the faculty at that prestigious Ivy League institution asked, Do sports matter? Are they relevant? Are they more than just fun and games?

The answer—an emphatic yes—is even more appropriate today than it was then. As an integral part of American society, sports provide insights to our history and culture and, for better or worse, help define who we are.

Sports In America is much more than a compilation of names, dates, and facts. Each volume chronicles accomplishments and expansions of the possible. Not just in the physical ability to perform, but in the ability to create goals and determine methods to achieve them. In this way, sports, the sweaty offspring of recreation and competition, resemble any other field of endeavor. I certainly wouldn't equate the race for a gold medal with the race to the moon, but the building blocks are the same: the intelligent application of talent, determination, research, practice, and hard work to a meaningful objective.

Sports matter because they show us in high definition. They communicate examples of determination, courage, and skill. They often embody a heroic human-interest story, overcoming poverty, injustice, injury, or disease. The phrase, "Sports is a microcosm of life," could also read "Life is a microcosm of sport."

Consider racial issues. When Jackie Robinson of the Brooklyn Dodgers broke through major league baseball's "color barrier" in 1947, the significance extended beyond the national pastime. Precisely because baseball was the national pastime, this epochal event reverberated throughout every part of American society.

To be sure, black stars from individual sports had preceded him (notably Joe Louis in boxing and Jesse Owens in track), and others would follow (Arthur Ashe in tennis and Tiger Woods in golf), but Robinson stood out as an important member of a team. He wasn't just playing with the Dodgers, he was traveling with them, living with them. He was a black member of a white athletic family. The benefits of integration could be appreciated far beyond the borough of Brooklyn. In 1997, Major League Baseball retired his "42" jersey number.

Sports have always been a laboratory for social awareness and change. Robinson integrated big league box scores eight years before the U.S. Supreme Court ordered the integration of public schools. The Paralympics (1960) and Special Olympics (1968) easily predate the Americans with Disabilities Act (1990). The mainstreaming of disabled athletes was especially apparent in 2007 when double amputee Jessica Long, 15, won the AAU Sullivan Award as America's top amateur. Women's official debut in the Olympic Games, though limited to swimming, occurred in 1912, seven years before they got the right to vote. So even if these sports were tardy in opening their doors, in another way, they were ahead of their times. And if it was necessary to break down some of those doors—Title IX support for female college athletes comes to mind—so be it. Basketball star Candace Parker won't let anyone keep her from the hoop.

Another area of importance, particularly as it affects young people, is substance abuse. High school, college, and professional teams all oppose the illegal use of drugs, tobacco, and alcohol. In most venues, testing is mandatory, and tolerance is zero. The confirmed use of performance enhancing drugs has damaged the reputations of such superstar athletes as Olympic sprinters Ben Johnson and Marion Jones, cyclist Floyd Landis, and baseball sluggers Manny Ramirez and Alex Rodriguez. Some athletes have lost their careers, or even their lives, to substance abuse. Conversely, other athletes have used their fame to caution young people about submitting to peer pressure or making poor choices.

Fans care about sports and sports personalities because they provide entertainment and self-identify—too often at a loss of priorities. One reason sports have flourished in this country is their support from governmental bodies. When a city council votes to help underwrite the cost of a sports facility or give financial advantages to the owners of a team, it affects the pocketbook of every taxpayer, not to mention the local ecosystem. When high schools and colleges allocate significant resources to athletics, administrators believe they are serving the greater good, but at what cost? Decisions with implications beyond the sports page merit everyone's attention.

In World War II, our country's sporting passion inspired President Franklin Roosevelt to declare that professional games should not be cancelled. He felt the benefits to the national psyche outweighed the risk of gathering large crowds at central locations. In 2001, another generation of Americans also continued to attend large-scale sports events because, to do otherwise, would "let the terrorists win." Being there, being a fan, yelling your lungs out, cheering victory and bemoaning defeat, is a cleansing, even therapeutic exercise. The security check at the gate is just part of the price of stepping inside. Even before there was a 9/11, there was a bloody terrorist assault at the Munich Olympic Games in 1972.

The popular notion "Sports build character" has been better expressed "Sports reveal character." We've witnessed too many coaches and athletes break rules of fair play and good conduct. The convictions of NBA referee Tim Donaghy for gambling and NFL quarterback Michael Vick for operating a dog-fighting ring are startling recent examples. We've even seen violence and cheating in youth sports, often by parents of a (supposed) future superstar. We've watched (at a safe distance) fans "celebrate" championships with destructive behavior. I would argue, however, that these flaws are the exception, not the rule, that the good of sports far outweighs the bad, that many of life's success stories took root on an athletic field.

Any serious examination of sports leads to the question of athletes as standards for conduct. Professional basketball star Charles Barkley created quite a stir in 1993 when he used a Nike shoe commercial to declare, "I am not paid to be a role model." The knee-jerk response argued, "Of course you are, because kids look up to you," but Barkley was right to raise the issue. He was saying that, in making lifestyle choices in language and behavior, young people should look elsewhere for role models, ideally to responsible parents or guardians.

The fact remains, however, that athletes occupy an exalted place in our society, especially when they are magnified in the mass media, sports talk radio, and the blogosphere. The athletes we venerate can be as young as a high school basketball player or as old as a Hall of Famer. (They can even be dead, as Babe Ruth's commercial longevity attests.) They are honored and coddled in a way few mortals are. Regrettably, we can be quick to excuse their excesses and ignore their indulgences. They influence the way we live and think: Ted Williams inspired patriotism as a wartime fighter pilot; Muhammad Ali's opposition to the Vietnam War on religious grounds, validated by the Supreme Court, encouraged the peace movement; Magic Johnson's contraction of the HIV/AIDs virus brought better understanding to a little-understood disease. No wonder we elect them—track stars, football coaches, baseball pitchers—to represent us in Washington. Meanwhile, television networks pay huge sums to sports leagues so their teams can pay fortunes for their services.

Indeed, it has always been this way. If we, as a nation, love sports, then we, quite naturally, will love the men and women who play them best. In return, they provide entertainment, release and inspiration. From the beginning of the 20th century until now, Sports In America is their story-and ours.

Larry Keith is the former Assistant Managing Editor of Sports Illustrated. *He created the editorial concept for* SI Kids *and was the editor of the official Olympic programs in 1996, 2000 and 2002. He is a former adjunct professor of Sports Journalism at Columbia University and is a member of the North Carolina Journalism Hall of Fame.*

INTRODUCTION
1960–1969

A NOT-SO-SUBTLE CHANGE TOOK place in the sports world in the 1960s: Where competing—striving for a championship—was the end-all early in the 1960s, cashing in—not just making a living playing sports, but getting rich doing it—crept in toward the end of the decade.

Athletes began to see themselves as entertainers who performed for money. Some observers saw that as an end to a simpler, more innocent time. Others saw it as overdue in an arena in which owners long had prospered at the expense of the athletes. That culture clash was a reflection of life in the 1960s, a period remembered for rebellion in the life-styles and attitudes of the younger generation—ideas that eventually crept into the mainstream and beyond.

Labor struggles were inevitable in the new sports-world order as the players organized by hiring union leaders to represent them in their dealings with team owners.

Race relations and issues of freedom were other themes of the decade. Heavy-weight boxing champion Cassius Clay, who became a Muslim and changed his name to Muhammad Ali, refused to register for the military draft in 1967 and was stripped of his heavyweight title. Black competitors used athletic venues to express their views against racism, such as at the 1968 Olympics.

Instances of the social strides that prove how sport mirrors society include the Boston Celtics. In 1966, they won an unprecedented eighth consecutive National Basketball Association (NBA) championship, after which the team named Bill Russell the NBA's first African-American coach.

Commercialism invaded sports during the decade, as corporate sponsors began paying Olympic athletes to sell their products. The ideal of amateurism—competing for sheer love of the sport—became a naive notion as big business invaded sports. The struggle to maintain

Decade of Protest *Anti-war sentiment in the United States was reflected in this protest in Berkeley, California.*

one's amateur status amid the increasing prize money came to a head in the Winter Olympics in 1968, the same year that tennis began allowing amateurs and pros to compete in the same tournaments.

New leagues sprouted up during the decade like tulips in springtime, with varying success, but always upsetting the status quo.

Despite suffering through embarrassing gambling and drug scandals, the racial tension of an integrated America on and off the fields, and the corruption resulting from big dollars coming into sports, sports fans still remember the memorable performances of the decade. Magnificent athletes such as Jim Brown, Jack Nicklaus, Wilma Rudolph, Sandy Koufax, Billie Jean King, Wilt Chamberlain, and others were at their height in the 1960s. These years also featured the staying power of such dynastic teams as the Celtics, the NFL's Green Bay Packers, and college basketball's University of California at Los Angeles (UCLA) Bruins.

The 1960s were one of the most revolutionary decades in American history. In this case, sports certainly imitated life.

1960

Rozelle Takes Over

In late January, NFL owners gathered in Miami Beach to pick the league's next commissioner. Bert Bell, who had been commissioner since 1946, died of a heart attack the previous October while attending a game between the Philadelphia Eagles and the Pittsburgh Steelers (the two teams he had previously owned).

After seven days and 22 ballots, the owners failed to break a deadlock between Austin Gunsel, who had been serving as acting commissioner since Bell's death, and Marshall Leahy, an attorney for the San Francisco 49ers. Finally, on the 23rd ballot, a surprise compromise candidate was voted in: Pete Rozelle, the 33-year general manager of the Los Angeles Rams.

Rozelle (1926–1996), who became the fourth commissioner in NFL history, was an inspired choice. He went on to do more to make the NFL successful than any player or coach in the league. During his term, from 1960 to 1989, the football league grew from 12 to 28 teams and merged with the AFL to create the Super Bowl.

The First Miracle on Ice

In a huge upset, the United States ice hockey team beat the Canadians, the Soviets, and the Czechs to win the Olympic gold medal at Squaw Valley, California, in February. Before the 1960 Games, the U.S. hockey team had never won a gold medal in the Winter Olympics.

First, the team beat Canada 2–1, as U.S. goalie Jack McCartan stopped 39 shots and Bob Cleary and Paul Johnson scored goals. Two days later, the United States recorded its first ice-hockey victory over a Soviet team when the Christian brothers, Billy and Roger, combined for a third-period goal that resulted in a 3–2 win.

After defeating the Soviet Union, the United States had to play Czechoslovakia at eight o'clock the next morning in the championship game. The Americans trailed the Czechs 4–3 entering the final period, and the U.S. players looked exhausted. During the break between periods, however, the captain of the Soviet team (the same team that had lost to the United States the day before) made a surprise visit to the Americans' dressing room. He urged the players to take extra oxygen to help them breathe easier.

Olympian Effort *American sprinter Wilma Rudolph (see page 11) shined in the 1960 Games in Rome, Italy.*

The Americans followed his advice and crushed the Czechs with six unanswered goals in the final period for a 9–4 victory to take home the gold. Roger Christian scored four goals in the game. Twenty years later, Dave Christian, Billy's son and Roger's nephew, played on the U.S. hockey team that won the gold medal at the 1980 Winter Olympics, in an equally stunning upset. (Another brother of Billy and Roger's, Gordon Christian, played for the U.S. team in the 1956 Games.)

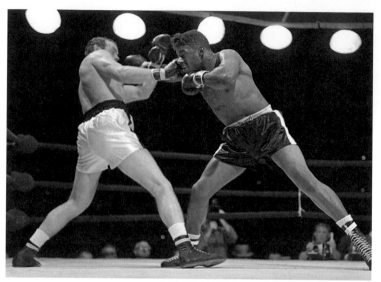

Fight Night *Floyd Patterson (right) and Ingemar Johansson duke it out in New York's Polo Grounds. Patterson regained the heavyweight title with a fifth-round knockout.*

Arnie Enlists His Army

In 1960, golfer Arnold Palmer (b.1929) was at the top of his form, winning eight of the 27 tournaments he entered, including the Masters and the U.S. Open. At the Masters, he attracted a crowd of admirers, dubbed Arnie's Army, who loved his winning ways and his "regular Joe" style of play. Palmer was a risky shotmaker, and sometimes played with his shirt untucked or his hair uncombed. He even talked to the fans in the gallery and signed autographs during play.

Palmer birdied (had one shot under par) the last two holes of the Masters to win by a stroke over Ken Venturi. He followed that victory with one of the most amazing comebacks ever seen in golf. On June 18, Palmer was seven shots behind leader Mike Souchak going into the final round of the U.S. Open at Cherry Hills Country Club in Denver, Colorado. Palmer's first shot of the par-four first hole landed on the green, and he got six birdies over the first seven holes to score a 30 on the first nine holes. He added a 35 on the last nine to finish with a 65 that vaulted him over 14 golfers to win the title. Palmer had come back from what seemed an impossible deficit to beat Jack Nicklaus (b.1940), the 20-year-old junior from Ohio State University, by two strokes.

Palmer, perhaps the most popular golfer ever, won 60 titles during his career and became the first player in his sport to earn $1 million. He won the Masters four times and the British Open two straight years. But more important, it was Palmer who made golf a sport for television. Prizes that were $5,000 are now more than $1 million. "Every golfer who makes his living off this game should thank the Lord daily that Arnold Palmer came along," long-time rival Chi Chi Rodriguez said. "Most of us would still be caddies."

Twice Is Nice

Floyd Patterson (1935–2006) became the first boxer to regain the world heavyweight championship when he knocked out the champion, Ingemar Johansson of Sweden, in the fifth round of their bout at New York's Polo Grounds. Patterson had lost his championship belt to Johansson during a title fight one year earlier, when Patterson was knocked down seven times in one round! In the rematch, on June 20, Patterson got his revenge. The 25-year-old New Yorker outboxed his bigger opponent, avoided Johansson's powerful right-hand punch, and connected with two devastating left hooks to floor the previously undefeated Swede.

The First Dream Team

Young fans today know "The Dream Team" as the United States basketball team for the 1992 Summer Olympic Games in Barcelona. That team, which included NBA players for the first time, featured stars such as Michael Jordan, Magic Johnson, and Larry Bird. It cruised to the gold medal, winning every game by a minimum of 32 points.

The 1992 squad wasn't the original Dream Team, though. The United States squad that traveled to Rome for the 1960 Olympics has often been called the best amateur basketball team ever assembled. Eight of the 12 players went on to play professionally in the NBA. Four made it to the Hall of Fame, including Jerry West (b.1938) and Oscar Robertson (b.1938). Robertson and Jerry Lucas (b.1940)—another future Hall of Famer who already had led his Ohio State Buckeyes to the National Collegiate Athletic Association (NCAA) championship in March—each averaged 17 points per game to pace this overpowering squad, which crushed each opponent by an average score of 102–60. The closest U.S. game in the tournament was a victory by 24 points!

In the championship game, the Americans sank the USSR, 81–57. The victory extended the U.S. Olympic team's winning streak to 36 games in a row.

Rudolph Leads the Way

Wilma Rudolph (1940–1994) could not walk when she was a youngster because she had polio, a disease that can cause paralysis. She wore a brace on her left leg until she was 12 years old. By the time she was 20, Wilma could run so fast that she was called the World's Fastest Woman. Rudolph won three gold medals at the 1960 Summer Olympic Games in Rome. She became the first American woman to win three golds in track and field at a single Olympics, setting world records in two of the events.

In the semifinal heat of the 100-meter dash, Rudolph tied the world record of 11.3 seconds, crossing the finish line a full three yards ahead of the runnerup—a huge margin of victory in so short a race. In the final heat, Rudolph claimed her first gold medal by winning in 11 seconds flat, but this record was not recognized

Decathlon

The decathlon is a 10-event track and field competition ("deca" means 10 in Greek) for men. This grueling competition is held over two days. The first day's events are the 100-meter dash, long jump, shot put, high jump, and 400-meter run. The events on the second day are the 110-meter hurdles, discus, pole vault, javelin, and 1,500-meter run. In the decathlon, athletes earn points based on their performance in each event. The athletes compete against one another, but they also try to perform as well as they can to earn the most points. The competitor who scores the most points in all the events combined wins. The winner of the decathlon in the Summer Olympic Games earns the title, "The World's Greatest Athlete."

1960

because the two-mile-an-hour wind at her back was over the Olympic limit.

In the 200-meter dash, Rudolph set a world record with a time of 22.0 seconds in a qualifying heat, the first time a woman broke the 23-second barrier. She then won her second gold medal with a time of 24.0 in the final (four-tenths of a second faster than her closest competitor), and she displayed a powerful finishing kick while anchoring the 4x100-meter relay team that set a world record.

The Rome Games were the first Olympics to be broadcast to millions of television viewers around the world and they were the first Olympics to be tele-vised live in the United States. Rudolph's success on the track did much to help women's athletics gain overall acceptance in America. Thousands of girls, inspired to "be like Wilma," joined local track clubs and then demanded competitive athletic opportunities in their schools, just like the boys. The seeds of Title IX, the landmark 1972 legislation that would vastly expand women's sports programs, had been planted.

Friendly Rivals

The favorites in the 10-event decathlon at the Rome Olympics were

Hero's Welcome   *Bill Mazeroski's teammates—and Forbes Field fans—greet Pittsburgh's second baseman after his dramatic home run ended the World Series.*

Rafer Johnson (b.1934) of the United States and C.K. Yang of Taiwan. Johnson, the silver medalist in the decathlon at the 1956 Olympics, and Yang were college friends who trained together while on the track and field team at the University of California at Los Angeles (UCLA).

After nine events, Johnson led Yang by only 67 points. As they entered the final event, the 1,500-meter race, Yang knew he had to beat Johnson by at least 10 seconds to win the gold. Yang won the race, but Johnson finished in a career best time of 4:49.7, which was only two seconds slower than Yang. Johnson won the gold medal with a record 8,392 points. Yang took the silver and became the first Taiwanese athlete to win an Olympic medal.

In 1984, Johnson was chosen to light the torch at the Opening Ceremonies of the Summer Olympics in Los Angeles.

The Series-Winning Homer

The 1960 World Series was one of the strangest, most exciting, unique, and entertaining in the rich and colorful history of the Fall Classic. When it was over, the N.L.'s Pittsburgh Pirates had upended the A.L.'s New York Yankees in seven games.

Looking at the statistics, the Series should have been won by the Yankees. The Bronx Bombers set a number of Series records—highest batting average (.338), most hits (91), most runs (55), and most runs batted in (54). But this October, the Yankees lost to the Pirates on one of the most dramatic endings in World Series history.

The Series was tied, three games each, after the Yankees routed the Pirates

Baseball by the Bay

The wrecking ball came down on Ebbets Field on February 23, as demolition began on what was the fabled home of the Brooklyn Dodgers for 44 seasons. The Dodgers moved to Los Angeles before the start of the 1958 season. Also in February, the Dodgers' owner, Walter O'Malley, completed his purchase of the Chavez Ravine area in Los Angeles, with plans to build his new baseball stadium there.

On April 12, 42,269 fans watched the former New York Giants (now the San Francisco Giants) beat the St. Louis Cardinals in the first game at San Francisco's new Candlestick Park. The park was so windy that pitcher Stu Miller was blown off the mound during the 1961 All-Star Game! The Giants played in Candlestick until 2000, when the team moved to its current facility, AT&T (originally Pac Bell and later SBC) Park.

in Forbes Field, 12–0 in Game Six. In the deciding seventh game, the Yankees rolled to a 7–4 lead, but the Pirates stormed back in the bottom of the eighth inning, scoring five runs to take a 9–7 advantage. In the top of the ninth inning, though, New York's Mickey Mantle (1931–1995) singled to score one run, then made a sensational base-running play to elude a tag, allowing the tying run to score.

Pittsburgh second baseman Bill Mazeroski (b.1936) was the leadoff batter in the bottom of the ninth. Ralph Terry, the fifth Yankee pitcher in the game, threw one ball and, on the second pitch, Mazeroski swung and blasted a high fly ball that cleared the left-field wall for a home run to win the Series for the Pirates.

Mazeroski jumped up and down, waving his cap in the air, like a robot gone wild. There were so many people on the field blocking his way by the time he rounded third base, he barely made

1960

it around to touch home plate. He did make it home, though, and the Pirates won, 10–9. The only other player to end a World Series with a homer is Joe Carter of the Toronto Blue Jays in game six of the 1993 Series against the Philadelphia Phillies.

California Dreaming

The NBA joined the expansion of professional sports to the West Coast, when the Lakers moved from Minneapolis to start the 1960–61 season in their new home, the 14,000-seat Los Angeles Memorial Sports Arena.

Los Angeles basketball fans were wowed by the moves of forward Elgin Baylor (b.1934), the first NBA player who seemed to defy gravity, "flying" in a way that Chicago Bulls star Michael Jordan later did in the 1980s and 1990s. The 6-foot-5 Baylor was an 11-time All-Star who averaged 27.4 points per game in the Lakers' first season in Los Angeles.

Baylor scored more than 60 points in a game three times in 1960–61, including an NBA-record 71-point performance on November 15, 1960, in the Lakers' 123–108 victory over the New York Knicks at Madison Square Garden. Baylor made 28 field goals and 15 free throws to break his own league mark of 64 points.

Football's Iron Man

With limited substitution in the 1930s and most of the 1940s, almost all NFL players were "two-way" players— that is, they played both offense and defense (and usually special teams, too). A

rule change in 1949 permitted free substitution and ushered in the era of specialization. By 1960, there was one full-time, two-way player left in the NFL: Chuck Bednarik (b.1925).

"The Iron Man," as he became known, played center on offense and linebacker on defense for the Philadelphia Eagles. A hard-hitting blocker and tackler, he was chosen All-Pro at both positions.

Bednarik, at 35, was the oldest man on the Eagles in 1960, and was a symbol of durability. The length of a regulation NFL game is 60 minutes, and Bednarik never seemed to leave the field, averaging 57.8 minutes per game. In the 1960 NFL Championship Game against the Green Bay Packers, held at Franklin Field in Philadelphia on December 26, Bednarik's performance inspired his teammates to a 17–13 victory.

While playing offense in the second quarter, Bednarik blocked blitzing defenders, allowing quarterback Norm Van Brocklin time to throw a touchdown pass. Then, while playing defense in the fourth period, he knocked down Green Bay's Jim Taylor at the nine-yard line on the final play. Bednarik's game-saving tackle gave Philadelphia its first championship in 11 years. He was on the field for nearly every play. The record book shows he played an incredible 58 minutes of the title game!

The Pack Is Back

Paul Hornung (b.1935) of the Green Bay Packers set the NFL single-season scoring record with 176 points: 15 touchdowns, 15 field goals, and 41 extra points. "The Golden Boy" added two more

Other Milestones of 1960

✔ There was a big problem as the date approached for the 1960 Winter Olympics to begin in Squaw Valley, California: no snow. The Piute, a local tribe of Native Americans, did a snow dance to help out, and it worked. A snowstorm came and saved the Games.

✔ The Charlotte Motor Speedway in Charlotte, North Carolina, opened on June 19 to host the World 600. Joe Lee Johnson won in a Chevy, averaging 107.75 mph.

Betsy Rawls

✔ Betsy Rawls set a women's golf record by winning her fourth U.S. Women's Open golf championship in July, scoring a four-round total of 292 for a one-stroke victory over Joyce Ziske at the Worcester (Massachusetts) Country Club. Rawls, who also won in 1951,

1953, and 1957, roared back from a seven-stroke deficit with a record-tying 68 in the third round. Mickey Wright equaled Rawls' mark of four U.S. Open victories in 1964.

✔ The year saw several baseball innovations. Bill Veeck, the maverick owner of the Chicago White Sox, was the first to put names on the back of his players' uniforms, above their numbers. Baltimore Orioles manager Paul Richards introduced an oversized mitt for his catchers' adventures with knuckleball pitcher Hoyt Wilhelm. The Cleveland Indians and Detroit Tigers made history on August 3 by trading managers. It had never been done before. Cleveland got Jimmy Dykes and Detroit got Joe Gordon.

field goals in the 1960 championship game, a loss to the Philadelphia Eagles.

The once-great Packers, making their first appearance in a title game since 1944, were beginning their resurgence under second-year head coach Vince Lombardi (1913–1970). In fact, this was the last time Lombardi's Packers ever lost a postseason game. Green Bay won NFL championships in 1961 and 1962, then three more from 1965 to 1967. The Packers also triumphed in the first two Super Bowl games, played following the 1966 and 1967 seasons.

Johnny U.

 Baltimore Colts' quarterback Johnny Unitas (1933–2002) extended his

NFL record-setting streak by throwing two touchdown passes in a game against the Detroit Lions on December 4. That gave Unitas at least one touchdown pass in 47 straight games! The streak, which stretched over four seasons, ended the following week in the same place where it started, the Los Angeles Coliseum.

Johnny U.'s record may stand forever. The closest anyone has ever come to it was the Miami Dolphins' Dan Marino (b.1961), who threw touchdown passes in 30 games in a row from 1985 to 1987.

With his crew cut and high-topped black cleats, Unitas was the personification of leadership at the quarterback position. He set 22 NFL passing records in an 18-year career with the Colts (1956 to 1972) and San Diego Chargers (1973).

1961

The Ageless Wonder

George Blanda, the quarterback for the Houston Oilers in the new American Football League, threw three touchdown passes and kicked a field goal to lead the Oilers to a 24–16 victory over the Los Angeles (now the San Diego) Chargers in the first AFL title game, played on the first day of 1961.

Blanda (b.1927) was a quarterback and kicker for 26 professional football seasons. He played in 340 games and did not stop playing until he was 48 years old—both pro football records! Blanda played his first 11 pro seasons in the NFL with the Chicago Bears. When Chicago decided to use him only as a kicker in 1959, he retired. The next year, however, the American Football League was formed, and Blanda joined the Oilers. During the next seven years in Houston, he passed for 19,149 yards and 165 touchdowns. In a game in 1961, Blanda set an AFL record by throwing seven touchdown passes in a 49–13 thrashing of the New York Titans (now the Jets).

A proven star like Blanda helped legitimize the new league. During the 1961 regular season, the 6-foot-2, 215-pounder threw 36 touchdown passes—a pro record that stood for 23 years until Dan Marino came along. Blanda's Oilers lit up the scoreboard, amassing 513 points in 14 games—100 more points than the AFL team with the next-best offense. Blanda was named the AFL's Player of the Year in 1961, when he helped Houston (now the Tennessee Titans) win its second straight AFL championship. The Oilers beat the Chargers 10–3 in the 1961 title game on December 24 in San Diego.

In 1967, Blanda was traded to the NFL's Oakland Raiders. In 1970, he came off the bench in five consecutive games to help the Raiders win or tie big games—at the age of 43!

Higher and Higher

On January 29, two high jumpers on different sides of the world reached new heights, as the world indoor record was set and broken.

John Thomas of the United States and Valeri Brumel of the Soviet Union both bettered the indoor record height of 7-feet-2 1/2 inches, which had been set by Thomas less than a year earlier, in March of 1960.

Two Titans *Roger Maris (left) and Mickey Mantle chased the homer record (page 21).*

At a track meet in Leningrad, Russia, Brumel jumped 7-feet-4 1/2 inches, setting a new world record. News that Brumel had added two inches to his former mark reached Thomas just as the 19-year-old student was preparing for a meet in Boston. "It must have been quite a jump," said Thomas, who then cleared 7-feet-3-inches, but did not attempt a record. Both jumpers broke the previous record. Brumel just broke it more!

Eight Is Enough

Bob Goalby drained eight birdies in a row in the final round of the St. Petersburg (Florida) Open to turn a two-shot deficit into a three-shot victory over Ted Kroll.

Goalby's timely birdie binge came over holes eight through 15 and set a Professional Golfers Association (PGA) record for the most birdies in a row. (The

The Boston Stranger

Talk about home field advantage! On November 3, the Boston Patriots beat the Dallas Texans 28–21, thanks to the defense of an anonymous Boston football fan. On the last play of the game, the Dallas quarterback, Cotton Davidson, threw the ball to a receiver in the end zone. A defender batted it away, ending the game. Unfortunately, the defender turned out to be a Boston fan who had sneaked onto the field. He immediately ran away before the referees saw him.

The Patriots played at old and decrepit Braves Field, once the home of perennial losers, the Boston Braves and the Boston Yanks—football teams during the 1940s that had failed for lack of fan support.

The New York Titans almost failed for the same reason. In their first season, played at the Polo Grounds, the Titans drew only 114,000 fans to their seven home games, so team owner Harry Wismer, a New York radio personality, began inflating the attendance figures announced to the media at each game. One cynical reporter, upon hearing Wismer's fuzzy math for a particular game, replied, "People must have showed up disguised as empty seats."

To avoid the embarrassment the Titans would have caused the entire league if the franchise had failed in New York (the country's largest media market), the AFL stepped in and assumed operation of the team. (Major League Baseball did the same thing with the Montreal Expos in 2002.) In 1962, a group led by Sonny Werblin purchased the Titans and changed the team name to the Jets. "Football is show business," said Werblin. "The game needs stars. Stars sell tickets." Three years later, Werblin put his money where his mouth was by signing University of Alabama quarterback Joe Namath (b.1943) for $427,000, the most ever paid to an athlete at the time. A nasty recruiting war between the AFL and NFL had begun.

old mark of seven was set by Tommy Bolt).

Several PGA players equaled Goalby's mark over the next four-plus decades, but no one managed nine consecutive birdies until 2009. That year, Mark Calcavecchia set the new record in the second round of the RBC Canadien Open. Calcavecchia shot 65 that day, but couldn't keep up the torrid pace and finished in a tie for eighth.

An Overtime Classic

The Cincinnati Bearcats outlasted the Ohio State Buckeyes 70–65 in overtime on March 25 to win the NCAA basketball championship for the first time in school history.

The final not only was a battle of Ohio powers, but also featured future basketball Hall of Famers on opposing sides. The Buckeyes, the defending NCAA champions, had a 31-game win streak and a lineup that included Jerry Lucas and John Havlicek (b.1940). On the other side were the University of Cincinnati Bearcats, who for the previous two years had expected to win a national championship behind Oscar Robertson (b.1938)— their star player who had since gone on to the NBA—only to fail in the semifinal game each time.

Lucas poured in 27 points for the Buckeyes, who kept the game close, but it was the Bearcats' swarming, switching defense that keyed their triumph. With 11 minutes left to play, Cincinnati was ahead by six points. Ohio State stormed back to go ahead by five, only to lose the lead before the end of regulation time, which ended tied at 61–61. The Bearcats got off quickly in overtime, and the Buckeyes never had an opportunity to draw even.

Memorial Day Champion

A.J. Foyt, a 26-year-old, tough-talking Texan, drove his Formula One racecar to a five-second victory over Eddie Sachs in the Indianapolis 500 on May 30.

Foyt (b.1935) and Sachs dueled for 300 miles in the 50th anniversary of the great race. Foyt pulled ahead with just 25 miles to go, but he needed a pit stop to repair a faulty fuel line. Sachs could have breezed to the finish line, but with three laps to go, he also was forced to make a pit stop to change a tire. Foyt zipped back on the track ahead of Sachs and took the checkered flag for the win.

Foyt, who was well on his way to making auto racing a mainstream sport, repeated his Indy victory three more times, in 1964, 1967, and 1977. Foyt won the Indy-car driving championship a record seven times and ran over anyone who got in his way. In 1972, he tried stock car racing and won the Daytona 500!

The Big Kahuna

Phil Edwards of the United States made a name for himself by catching a wave. Edwards became the first person to ride the Banzai Pipeline, one of Hawaii's best surfing areas. At the Banzai Pipeline, waves hit two sets of submerged reefs that slow the bottom of the wave,

making the front rise up and get steeper. Then, the top of the wave comes crashing forward, creating a tube of air inside that brave surfers try to ride.

Surfing competitions became serious as surfboard designs improved and surfers' abilities improved. In 1964, the first official world championships were held at Manly Beach in Australia. And in 1966, the first Duke Kahanamoku Invitational was held in Hawaii. In 1969, the Duke Kahanamoku Invitational awarded $1,000 in prize money to the winner. (Duke Kahanamoku was a Hawaiian who won a gold medal for the United States in the 100-meter freestyle swim at the 1912

Speedy Champ *A.J. Foyt, one of the legends of American motor racing, celebrates after winning the Indianapolis 500 in May, the first of four he would win in his great career.*

19

Smile for the Camera! *Kansas City Chiefs tackle, Dave Hill, is filmed before his team played the Green Bay Packers in the first Super Bowl in January of 1967. TV and sports made great strides in the decade.*

The Big Picture

This was a breakthrough year in the marriage of television and sports. *ABC's Wide World of Sports*, a weekly anthology show produced by Roone Arledge (1931–2002), hit the airwaves for the first time on April 29 with Jim McKay as host. The debut telecast featured two track events: the Penn Relays from Franklin Field in Philadelphia, and the Drake Relays from Des Moines, Iowa. *ABC's Wide World of Sports* began as a 20-week series; it is now the longest-running sports program in the history of television. The show, which covered such diverse fare as downhill skiing in Switzerland and figure skating in the Soviet Union, whetted Americans' tastes for nontraditional sports.

The power of television was not lost on the NFL's Pete Rozelle. He had been working on lucrative television contracts since he was elected the league's commissioner in 1960 (see page 8). He had seen football's future—through the television camera. Rozelle realized that if he could represent all the teams in one television package, the league would have more bargaining power with the networks.

First, Rozelle had to convince the successful team owners that it was in their best interest to share television revenues equally, even with struggling teams. In the short run, they might not make as much money. But in the long run, all the teams would benefit, making the league stronger. With this accomplished, in 1961 Rozelle helped fight for a federal law exempting football from future monopoly charges. This way the league could act as one unit instead of as individual teams.

Olympics and later made surfing popular around the world.)

Many surfers were unhappy that surfing was becoming a professional sport. They felt surfing was an art form, and that it was impossible to judge if one surfer had done better than another. These men and women were known as "soul surfers," because they preferred to surf for the good of their souls, rather than for money or fame.

In the early 1960s, the number of surfers around the world grew from the thousands into the millions. Motion pictures and popular music helped. A series of successful movies featured a young California girl named Gidget who loved to surf. And people all over the country heard the Beach Boys sing songs about California and surfing. In one of their most popular songs, "Surfin' USA," the Beach Boys sang, "Catch a wave and you're sitting on top of the world!"

In 1962, the NFL signed a two-year contract with CBS for $4.5 million a year. Then, during the merger with the AFL, the leagues negotiated a four-year contract with both CBS and NBC for $9.5 million. By 1969, the newly combined league signed a $150-million contract with ABC. The network, at Rozelle's suggestion, televised 13 NFL regular-season Monday night football games for the next three years. Howard Cosell (1925–1995), Don Meredith (b. 1938), and Frank Gifford (b.1930) became the network's celebrity broadcast crew. Monday nights during the fall and winter would never be the same again.

New Home Run King

 In 1927, New York Yankees legend Babe Ruth blasted an incredible 60 home runs—more than any other *team* in the American League had. The possibility of anyone breaking Ruth's mark was almost unthinkable, but in 1961 not one, but two, Yankees launched an assault on Ruth's hallowed mark. In the end, outfielder Roger Maris (1934–1985) set a new single-season record of 61 home runs; teammate Mickey Mantle (1931–1995) finished with with 54.

Mantle started out red-hot, but injuries forced him to drop out of the race in mid-September. Maris pulled ahead in the middle of September, but the pressure of making a run at one of baseball's most cherished records was so intense that it made Maris's hair fall out in clumps.

On October 1, the final day of the season, the Boston Red Sox were visiting Yankee Stadium. In the bottom of the fourth inning, Red Sox pitcher Tracy

Bleacher Creatures

Only 23,154 fans attended the Yankees' final game of the 1961 season, but many crowded into the right-field stands, hoping to catch the ball if Roger Maris hit home run number 61. A California restaurant owner had offered to pay $5,000 for the ball.

Sal Durante, a 19-year-old truck driver from Coney Island, New York, was the lucky fan who caught the ball as it dropped into the stands, 10 rows back and about 10 feet to the right of the Yankee bullpen.

Durante received congratulatory pats on the back from the delighted patrons. Contrast that with the legal battle to determine who owns Barry Bonds' record-setting 73rd home run ball. A trial in San Francisco Superior Court involved two 37-year-old men. Alex Popov—who said he caught Bonds' historic homer on October 7, 2001, and held onto it amidst a pack of fans until it was torn from his hands—and Patrick Hayashi, who claimed that the ball rolled loose during the melee, and he plucked it from the ground. A judge ruled that the two men had to split the proceeds from the ball after it was put up for auction (it fetched $450,000). Obviously, the zeal of sports collectors had grown in direct proportion to the skyrocketing value of sports collectibles.

1961

Stallard was behind in the count with two balls and no strikes to Maris when he served up a fastball. Maris connected and stroked it into section 33 of the rightfield bleachers. The hit was Maris's 61st home run for 1961—one more than Ruth hit in 1927—though the Babe did it in 10 fewer games.

Maris' home run also was the 240th of the season for the Yankees, another record that stood 34 years. More importantly, the "M&M Boys," as Mantle and Maris were called, helped the Yankees win the world championship. New York rolled to 109 victories during the regular season, leaving Detroit and its 101 wins a full eight games behind. Then, in the World Series in October, the Yankees easily beat the Cincinnati Reds four games to one.

Maris held the record 37 years—longer than Ruth had held it—until Mark McGwire (b.1963) of the St. Louis Cardinals surpassed the mark with 70 homers in 1998. His record was subsequently broken when the San Francisco Giants' Barry Bonds (b.1964) hit 73 home runs in the 2001 season.

Other Milestones of 1961

✔ In May, the Chicago Blackhawks defeated the Detroit Red Wings in six games to win the National Hockey League's (NHL) Stanley Cup championship. The Blackhawks finished in third place in the six-team NHL during the regular season, then stunned the Montreal Canadiens in six games in the semifinals to end that team's five-year run as champs. Chicago won the Stanley Cup for the first time in 23 years.

✔ On May 9, Jim Gentile of the Baltimore Orioles used his bat to make baseball history. Three weeks after Soviet astronaut Yuri Gagarin defied gravity to become the first man in space, Gentile defied baseball probabilities. Playing against the Minnesota Twins, the first baseman pounded a home run with the bases loaded in the first inning. Then he did it again in the second inning. Gentile set a major-league record by knocking in eight runs in two at-bats. The Orioles won 13–5. (Fernando Tatis did the unthinkable on April 23, 1999.

Pvt. Paul Hornung

The St. Louis Cardinals third baseman hit two grand slam home runs off Los Angeles Dodgers pitcher Chan Ho Park in the third inning of a game at Dodger Stadium. Tatis is the only batter to drive in eight runs in one inning.)

✔ Paul Hornung, on leave from the Army to play for the Green Bay Packers, scored 19 points—still a record for an NFL title game—as Green Bay won its seventh league title by routing the New York Giants 37–0 in Green Bay December 31. Hornung scored a touchdown on a six-yard run in the first half and kicked four extra points and three field goals. After this game, Green Bay became known as "Titletown, U.S.A."

Ford Keeps Rolling

This was not a good year for Babe Ruth. After Roger Maris surpassed the Babe's season record for home runs, Whitey Ford (b.1928) knocked him out of the World Series record book.

As a Boston Red Sox pitcher, the Babe pitched 29 consecutive scoreless innings in the World Series. But after pitching two shutouts of the Pittsburgh Pirates in 1960, Ford added 14 shutout innings of the Cincinnati Reds in the 1961 World Series to extend his streak to a record 32 consecutive scoreless innings.

Ford had a 25–4 record during the 1961 season, won two more games in the World Series, and received the Cy Young Award (for best pitcher) at a time when pitchers in both leagues competed for only one award. His lifetime record of 236–106 gave him the best career percentage of games won (.690) of any pitcher since 1900. And his most impressive performances came when it counted most—in the World Series. The lefthander still holds several important World Series pitching records, including most wins (10) and most losses (eight). Ford, who was known as "The Chairman of the Board," appeared in 11 Series, had the most Series starts (22), and had the most opening-game starts (eight). He pitched the most innings (146), had the most strikeouts (94), and the most walks (34).

One Tough Coach

The University of Alabama Crimson Tide football team posted a perfect 11–0 record and won the national title for the first time under legendary coach Paul "Bear" Bryant (1913–1983). The miracle worker in the houndstooth hat transformed foundering programs wherever he went, first at the University of Kentucky, then at Texas A & M. In 1958, he arrived in Tuscaloosa, Alabama, to take over a Crimson Tide team that had fallen to 2–7–1 the previous season.

In Bryant's 25 years at Alabama, his teams went on to win six national titles and 15 bowl games, and finish four seasons with an undefeated record. On November 28, 1981, Bryant earned win number 315, surpassing Amos Alonzo Stagg (1862–1965) as the winningest college football coach in history. Asked about the record, Bryant said, "All I did was stick with it." His 323rd and final victory was a 21–15 win over the University of Illinois on December 29, 1982, in the Liberty Bowl. Four weeks later, on January 26, 1983, the 69-year-old Bryant died of a heart attack. In 38 years as head coach at the University of Maryland, Kentucky, Texas A&M, and Alabama, the Bear coached only one team that posted a losing season.

1962

The Soaring Marine

Heading down the runway on his attempt to become the first man to vault 16 feet, John Uelses thought the height looked insurmountable. After all, it had been 29 years since the 15-foot barrier had been shattered; for a long time, 16 feet was unthinkable. But the 1960s introduced the fiberglass pole, and on February 2, Uelses soared 16 feet and one-quarter inch during competition in the Millrose Games at New York's Madison Square Garden.

The 24-year-old Marine missed on his first two attempts at the magical 16-foot height, but he easily cleared the bar on his final vault. "I just can't believe it," he said. "Even when I was pounding down the runway I was thinking, 'I'll never make it.'"

The fiberglass pole eventually replaced the wooden one, which had much less spring, and effectively rewrote the record books by enabling vaulters to soar ever higher. (By 1963, the 17-foot mark was shattered.) Three weeks after Uelses' feat, American astronaut John Glenn—really rocketing into space—successfully orbited the earth.

The Hershey Hundred

On March 2, Wilt Chamberlain (1936–1999) of the Philadelphia Warriors put on the greatest one-man show in NBA history. Chamberlain poured in 100 points as Philadelphia beat the New York Knicks, 169–147, in Hershey, Pennsylvania. No one else has ever come close to Chamberlain's amazing single-game record.

Right from the start, Philadelphia sped to a 19–3 lead. Chamberlain had 13 of those 19 points, including seven consecutive free throws—which he usually had trouble sinking. His early luck proved a good omen. By the end of the first quarter, Chamberlain had 23 of his team's 42 points. He had 41 points by halftime, when the Warriors led 79–68.

In the third period, Chamberlain was eight for eight from the foul line and made 10 baskets for a 28-point quarter. He had 69 points in the game's first 36 minutes. Chamberlain broke his own single-game record by reaching 79 points with more than seven minutes remaining (he had scored 78 points in a game against the Los Angeles Lakers in December, 1961). His tally stood at 89 points with five minutes

Century Mark *Wilt Chamberlain set an all-time record with his 100-point night.*

left to play. But then he failed to score for more than two minutes! He quickly dropped in three free throws and two jumpers. Now he had 96 points. The 4,124 fans in Hershey Arena were yelling, "Give it to Wilt!"—which the Warriors did.

Chamberlain had 98 points with 1:27 to play, and the crowd was frantic to see him reach the century mark. But the next three times he got the ball, he shot and missed. The Knicks were now stalling to avoid being embarrassed, and they were fouling other Warriors to keep the ball away from Chamberlain.

New York tried a collapsing defense around the big man (putting two or three defenders on him whenever he got near the basket). There would be no denying

The Big Dipper

An individual scoring 50 points in a pro basketball game is a rare feat usually accomplished only a handful of times in a given NBA season. Imagine, then, how extraordinary Wilt Chamberlain's 1961–62 season was. The Philadelphia Warriors' star *averaged* 50.4 points per game that season.

A powerful slam-dunker, Chamberlain was called "The Big Dipper." The 7-foot-1, 275-pound center was also known as "Wilt the Stilt." Chamberlain's career scoring average of 30.06 points per game is second only to Michael Jordan's 30.12. His 31,419 points still rank him third in lifetime scoring, behind Kareem Abdul-Jabbar and Karl Malone. His average of 22.9 rebounds per game remains an NBA record.

Chamberlain finished the 1961–62 season with 4,029 points, making him the only player to score more than 4,000 points in a season. In 46 of his team's 80 games in the regular season, the Stilt scored 50 or more points. But he was not named the NBA's Most Valuable Player for the season. That honor went to Bill Russell of the Boston Celtics. Russell used his defensive skills to lead the Celtics to the NBA title. Chamberlain and Russell had one of the most famous rivalries in NBA history.

In 1960, Chamberlain set the all-time NBA record of 55 rebounds in a game against the Celtics. Chamberlain left the NBA's Eastern Division when the Warriors moved to San Francisco in 1962, but he returned in 1965 to play for the Philadelphia 76ers. In the 1966–67 season, Chamberlain led the 76ers to 68 wins (then a record) and the NBA title. The next season, Chamberlain focused on his passing and became the first center to lead the NBA in assists.

Chamberlain was traded to the Los Angeles Lakers in 1968 and stayed with the team until his retirement. His final triumph came at age 35 in 1971–72: Chamberlain led the NBA in field-goal percentage (the percentage of shots that are successful) and rebounding, and helped lead his team to 69 wins (then a record) and the league championship.

Chamberlain on this night, however. Finally, with 46 seconds remaining, Chamberlain got the ball a few feet from the basket and slammed home a final dunk for 100 points in the game. In all, Chamberlain made 36 of 63 field goals. Usually a horrendous free-throw shooter, he even made 28 of 32 free throws!

25 Deadly Blows

Emile Griffith regained the world welterweight boxing championship from Benny "Kid" Paret on March 24 at Madison Square Garden in New York. Griffith stopped Paret in round 12 with a devastating flurry of punches. After backing Paret against the ropes, Griffith let fly with 25 consecutive blows before the referee stepped in. Paret underwent emergency brain surgery, but the 25-year-old Cuban never regained consciousness and died on April 3. Paret's death led to a public outcry that boxing was too dangerous and too violent, and should be banned as a spectator sport.

Lovable Losers

The Brooklyn Dodgers and the New York Giants dealt a double blow to baseball fans in the Big Apple when both teams left New York City to play on the West Coast (the Dodgers in Los Angeles and the Giants in San Francisco) beginning with the 1959 season. It was not until the arrival of the expansion New York Mets in 1962 that the void was filled.

To manage their new team, Mets owners turned to a baseball legend: 72-year-old Casey Stengel (1890–1975), who as a player and manager had been a New York fixture for almost 50 years.

"The Old Professor" had led the New York Yankees to 10 pennants and seven World Series titles in 12 years as manager, from 1949 to 1960. But with the Mets, he was the manager of one of the worst, but best-loved, teams in history. The 1962 Mets, who captured the hearts of New York baseball fans, won 40 games and lost 120. Stengel skillfully deflected any criticism as only he could. After the Mets set a major-league record for futility by losing game number 120, Stengel addressed his players in the locker room. "Men," he said, "no one person is responsible. This was truly a total team effort."

Stengel was best known for his skill as a manger and for his colorful language—a variation of English that came to be called "Stengelese."

The Green Team

The Boston Celtics, coached by Red Auerbach, won a then-record fourth straight NBA title, defeating the Los Angeles Lakers, 110–107, in game seven of the finals behind a 44-rebound, 30-point performance by Bill Russell on April 18. The Celtics surpassed the Minneapolis Lakers' record of three straight championships (from 1952 to 1954). The Celtics went on to win four more NBA titles, run-

ning their record streak to eight in a row. Nine future Hall of Famers played on Auerbach's championship teams, including K.C. Jones, Sam Jones, John Havlicek, Tom Heinsohn, and Frank Ramsey.

A Triple Threat

Oscar Robertson of the Cincinnati Royals, one of the greatest all-around players in NBA history, averaged a triple-double: 30.8 points, 12.5 rebounds, and 11.4 assists—per game!—during the 1961–62 regular season.

Robertson mastered every phase of the game: shooting, dribbling, passing, rebounding, defense, and teamwork. "The Big O" grew up in Indiana and played college

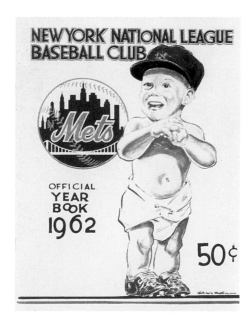

Baby Steps *The New York Mets first took the field in 1962. The club's infant years were not very successful.*

1962

basketball at the University of Cincinnati. He was drafted by the NBA's Cincinnati Royals (now the Sacramento Kings) in 1960. He led the league in assists and was named Rookie of the Year. Three seasons later, he was league MVP. Cincinnati traded Robertson to the Milwaukee Bucks early in the 1969–1970 season. There, he teamed with Lew Alcindor (who later changed his name to Kareem Abdul-Jabbar) to lead the Bucks to the NBA title.

Robertson retired as the highest-scoring guard of all time (with 26,710 points) and as the assists leader, too (with 9,887). He was elected to the Naismith Memorial Basketball Hall of Fame in 1979.

Nicklaus Breaks Through

 Jack Nicklaus beat heavily favored Arnold Palmer in an 18-hole playoff

on June 17 to become the first rookie golfer ever to win the United States Open. Nicklaus was the victor in a duel that tested emotions as well as golfing skills.

The tournament was played at Oakmont Country Club in Pennsylvania, Palmer's home state. The popular Palmer is from nearby Latrobe, Pennsylvania, and the partisan gallery constantly called "Come on, Arnie," and hooted at the 22-year-old Nicklaus. But Nicklaus, already a two-time winner of the U.S. Amateur title, was not rattled by the hostile fans. He jumped to a four-stroke lead after six holes of the playoff and coasted to a 71—three strokes better than Palmer.

Déja Vu

 Eleven years to the day after Bobby Thomson's famous home run lifted

Say Hey! *Willie Mays (batting) and the Giants won a thrilling race for the N.L. pennant, but lost to the New York Yankees in the World Series.*

Other Milestones of 1962

✔ In college football, the University of Southern California streaked to an undefeated record and the national title, the first for coach John McKay. The Trojans' perfect record was sorely tested in the Rose Bowl on New Year's Day of 1963 as the University of Wisconsin staged a furious comeback but fell short in USC's 42–37 win (see page 30).

Patterson vs. Liston

✔ Washington Senators pitcher Tom Cheney set a Major League Baseball record by striking out 21 Baltimore Orioles in the Senators' 16-inning, 2–1 win at Baltimore on September 12.

✔ Heavyweight boxing champion Floyd Patterson was knocked out by Sonny Liston in the first round of their championship fight at Chicago's Comiskey Park on September 25.

✔ The New York Giants' Y.A. Tittle tied an NFL record by tossing seven touchdown passes in a 49–34 win over the Washington Redskins on October 28.

✔ The National Basketball Association expanded to the West Coast, with the Philadelphia Warriors moving to San Francisco. Basketball fans near the Golden Gate Bridge were excited to watch the Warriors' star, 7-foot-1 center Wilt Chamberlain.

✔ Maury Wills, the Dodgers' speedy shortstop, set a big-league record by stealing 104 bases in 1962. Ty Cobb held the old mark with 96 thefts way back in 1915.

✔ On December 23, the Dallas Texans won the American Football League championship by overcoming the Houston Oilers after two minutes, 54 seconds of the second overtime period, 20–17. At the time, it was the longest pro football game ever played.

✔ The Green Bay Packers beat the New York Giants 16–7 at New York's Yankee Stadium on December 30 to win their second straight NFL title.

the Giants (then based in New York) past the Dodgers (then based in Brooklyn), the Giants did it to their fiercest rivals again, mounting a ninth-inning rally in the third game of a playoff to win the N.L. pennant and reach the World Series.

The Dodgers (now in Los Angeles) took a 4–2 lead into the top of the ninth inning against the visiting Giants (now in San Francisco) in the deciding game of the 1962 playoff. But San Francisco utilized four walks, an error, a wild pitch, and a sacrifice fly to mount a four-run rally and win the game 6–4.

Unfortunately for the Giants, the World Series also was a repeat of 1962. Beating the Dodgers meant a date with the Yankees in the World Series, and, just like 11 years earlier, the Yankees won.

The Series went seven games, with New York winning the finale 1–0 when second baseman Bobby Richardson caught Willie McCovey's liner with two on and two out in the ninth inning.

1963

No Household Name

Until 1965, the Associated Press crowned its national champion before the bowl season. That didn't make the Rose Bowl on New Year's Day 1963 any less memorable.

The USC Trojans entered the game already having been crowned national champs, and they looked the part while building a 42–14 lead against the second-ranked University of Wisconsin Badgers with 12 minutes remaining. Wisconsin rallied behind quarterback Ron VanderKelen's passing—he completed 33 of 48 passes for 401 yards in the game—to stage a furious rally that fell just short in a 42–37 loss.

On August 2, VanderKelen was again at the center of a wild and crazy game. Between 1934 and 1976, the defending NFL championship team played an exhibition game every year against a team of college all-stars. Sometimes, the students won. In 1963, the College All-Stars beat the Green Bay Packers! With three minutes remaining in the game, VanderKelen fired a 74-yard touchdown pass to former Wisconsin teammate Pat Richter for the 20–17 upset at Chicago's Soldier Field.

Football's Ups and Downs

On January 9, Paul Brown (1908–1991), founder of the Cleveland Browns of the old All-America Football Conference and the NFL, the winner of seven league titles, and the man after which the team was named, was fired as coach and general manager by the club's new owner, former television and advertising executive Art Modell, who had purchased the club in 1961.

Under new coach Blanton Collier, Cleveland won 10 of 14 games. Browns fullback Jim Brown (b.1936) ran for a then-record 1,863 yards in 1963—103 yards more than a mile—while becoming the career leader in rushing yardage. Brown brought his career total to 9,322 yards, surpassing the old record of 8,378 yards set by Joe Perry, who starred for the San Francisco 49ers and the Baltimore Colts from 1950 to 1962.

In November, the NFL played while the nation grieved. Football fans were angry at the NFL's decision to play its regularly scheduled Sunday games just three days after President John F. Kennedy's assassination in Dallas, Texas. Outraged fans pointed out that games in the NBA, NHL, and AFL were cancelled, but NFL commissioner Pete Rozelle, who said, "Football was Mr. Kennedy's game," announced the games would be played. Rozelle later called this his worst decision as commissioner.

By season's end, New York Giants quarterback Y.A. Tittle (b.1926) had thrown for 3,145 yards and a single-season record 36 touchdowns—three more than the record he set in 1962. The Giants, 11–3 during the regular season, faced the Chicago Bears in the NFL Championship Game at Wrigley Field in Chicago on December 29. The Giants lost 14–10—the third year in a row they lost the title game.

Black Eye for Golden Boy

On April 17, commissioner Pete Rozelle suspended two of the NFL's top players for gambling. Green Bay Packers halfback Paul Hornung and Detroit Lions defensive tackle Alex Karras were suspended indefinitely for betting on league games. In making the announcement, Rozelle stressed that neither player bet against his own team or gave less than 100 percent during games.

Hornung was nicknamed "Golden Boy" because of his blond hair, good looks, and sparkling talent. As a quarterback at the University of Notre Dame, he won the Heisman Trophy in 1956, the only time a player from a losing team has taken home the prestigious award. He joined the Packers in 1957 and sparked the team to NFL titles in 1961 and 1962. Hornung was a triple threat, meaning he could run, pass, and kick. He led the NFL in scoring for three seasons, including a

The Golden Bear *Jack Nicklaus (page 32) won two majors in 1963 (the Masters and PGA Championship) on his way to amassing the highest total of such titles in golf history.*

1963

record 176 points in 1960. Karras bitterly criticized Rozelle's punishment, but Hornung admitted he was guilty and never complained publicly about his suspension. The suspensions were lifted at the end of the 1963 season, but the integrity of professional football was assured for much longer.

Hornung and Karras returned to their respective teams for the 1964 season. But for Hornung, age and the year off had taken their toll. He led the team in scoring once again, but he rushed for just 415 yards. He never again played like the Golden Boy of old, and his career ended with an injury two years later.

Karras played until the early 1970s and then became a television commentator on Monday night football from 1974 to 1976. He also appeared in films, notably the Mel Brooks comedy *Blazing Saddles*, and starred on the TV sitcom *Webster* with Emmanuel Lewis in the title role.

Big Win for Small School

The University of Cincinnati Bearcats had their third straight NCAA men's basketball title all but won, but tiny Loyola of Chicago broke through for an unbelievable overtime victory, 60–58. The Loyola Ramblers missed 13 of their first 14 shots and trailed by 15 points with 12 minutes to play. But the Ramblers' frenetic style eventually forced the cautious Bearcats into ball-handling errors and defensive fouls. The once-huge Cincinnati lead dwindled: 48–39, 48–43, 50–48. Loyola captain and All-American Jerry Harkness hit the tying basket with five seconds remaining to send the game into overtime. In the extra minutes, Loyola's Vic Rouse grabbed an offensive rebound and laid it in at the buzzer for a 60–58 victory.

Nicklaus Makes His Mark

Jack Nicklaus, who won his first pro golf tournament at the 1962 U.S. Open (see page 28), proved to be the rising young star on the Professional Golfers' Association (PGA) circuit. In 1963, Nicklaus added the Masters and PGA titles to his growing list of credentials. By taming the Masters' Augusta National course with a two-under-par 286 that placed him one stroke ahead of Tony Lema and two ahead of three-time-winner Sam Snead, the 23-year-old Nicklaus became the youngest winner of the prestigious tournament, a distinction he held until 21-year-old Tiger Woods (b.1975) won in 1997. To capture the first of his five PGA Championship trophies, Nicklaus posted a final-round 68 in Dallas, Texas, for a 279 total. He overcame a three-stroke deficit to win.

Although Arnold Palmer did not win a major tournament in 1963, he won enough to become the first golfer to top the $100,000 mark in single-season winnings, finishing the year with $128,230. Palmer made golf a big-time sport in America by turning what was considered a country-club sport into one that had the tension of football and the suspense of baseball. Palmer boldly attacked every course he played; he visibly agonized over sliced drives and punched his fist into the air after sinking clutch putts. "Arnie's Army" of fans loved it, even when he was not in contention. No matter where or when he played, his galleries were the largest and loudest, cheering every birdie with a loud "Charge!"

Seventeen Is the New 16

Just 18 months after John Uelses became the first pole vaulter to clear 16 feet (see page 24), John Pennel shattered the 17-foot mark on August 24 in Miami, Florida.

Pennel, using a fiberglass pole that made the increasingly higher marks possible, vaulted 17-feet-0 3/4 inches at the Florida Gold Coast Amateur Athletic Union meet in his hometown. It was the sixth time in 1963 that Pennel upped the world pole-vault record.

Party Crasher

Some fighters are boxers. Sonny Liston (1932–1970) was a puncher, and his sledge-hammer right hand was as intimidating as his menacing scowl. Liston's reputation for being downright nasty was enhanced when he retained his world heavyweight championship with a first-round knockout of former champ Floyd Patterson on July 22.

But Liston hardly had time to savor this victory—his 35th win in 36 fights—when another young contender, former Olympic champion Cassius Clay, began showboating for the ringside crowd.

Clay screamed, "I'm the uncrowned champ. Liston is the tramp, I'm the champ." The next year, Clay (who later changed his name to Muhammad Ali) pulled off one of the most shocking upsets in boxing history (see page 38).

End of the Road for ABL

When American Basketball League commissioner Abe Saperstein, the founder of the Harlem Globetrotters, announced that the league was calling it quits after just a season and a half, some prominent players were made available for the NBA to pick up: Connie Hawkins, the ABL's scoring leader in its only season, Dick Barnett, Bill Bridges, and Jerry Lucas. Lucas had signed to play with the Cleveland Pipers, a team that withdrew from the ABL after winning the league's first championship, only to be denied permission to join the NBA.

Although the eight-team ABL was a failure, Saperstein's Globetrotters are still famous around the world. Saperstein is the only individual associated with the team in the Basketball Hall of Fame, but the Hall honors the Globetrotters with a special exhibit.

Instant Replay

The first television instant replay occurred on December 7, during the annual Army-Navy college football game, which Navy won 21–15. Tony Verna (what other initials could he have?) was a young director for CBS who introduced the new concept of showing a play again immediately after it took place.

With a Cotton Bowl bid at stake for the winner, number-two-ranked Navy led Army 21–7 in the fourth quarter. Less than seven minutes remained when Army's Rollie Stichweh faked a handoff, scored on a bootleg (a quick run to the outside by the quarterback), and then ran for a

33

Field Admiral *Navy quarterback Roger Staubach won the Heisman Trophy as the nation's top college player. He then went into military service, postponing the start of what would be a Hall of Fame career.*

Anchors Aweigh

Quarterback Roger Staubach (b.1942) of the U.S. Naval Academy won the Heisman Trophy as college football's best player in December. But the pros had to wait. Because of his Navy commitment, Staubach served his country for four years before joining the pros. He played for the NFL's Dallas Cowboys from 1969 to 1979, leading them to Super Bowl titles in 1971 and 1977.

Staubach was the Navy's most decorated athlete until David Robinson (b.1965) won three Olympic gold medals as a member of the United States basketball Dream Teams in 1988, 1992, and 1996. Robinson, too, delayed his move to the pros to fulfill his Navy commitment. He played for the San Antonio Spurs for 14 seasons before retiring in 2003.

Canton or Bust

The Pro Football Hall of Fame at Canton, Ohio, was dedicated in September with the induction of 17 charter members. The original inductees—a combination of players, coaches, and commissioners—were Sammy Baugh, Bert Bell, Joe Carr, Dutch Clark, Red Grange, George Halas, Mel Hein, Pete "Fats" Henry, Cal Hubbard, Don Hutson, Curly Lambeau, Tim Mara, George Marshall, Johnny "Blood" McNally, Bronko Nagurski, Ernie Nevers, and Jim Thorpe. Of the 17 immortalized, 12 were still alive at the time.

It's interesting to note that Cal Hubbard is also in the Baseball Hall of Fame (he is the only man in both the football and baseball halls). While still playing

two-point conversion, pulling Army to within six points. In its broadcast of the game, CBS made Stichweh's touchdown run television's first instant replay.

The idea of seeing a play again just seconds after it happened was so new that Lindsey Nelson, who was announcing the game, had to warn viewers. "This is not live!" Nelson screamed into the microphone. "Ladies and gentlemen, Army did not score again!"

The touchdown was the only time that day CBS used instant replay, because the replay pictures were not very clear. Still, the innovation forever changed the way we watch televised sports.

football, Hubbard started working as an umpire in baseball games, and he became an American League umpire in the mid-1930s. He worked as an umpire for 20 years and was considered one of the best. "I was so big," the former NFL tackle once said, "the other fellows were afraid to argue with me."

Meet Ms. Wright

When television began broadcasting women's golf in 1963, audiences often saw the Wright stuff; Mickey Wright (b.1935) won a record 13 times that year. She also won 10 tournaments in two other years. Wright won 82 career titles to rank second on the all-time list.

Using a swing that experts called perfect, the tall, long-hitting blonde from San Diego, California, won 13 majors in her career, including the U.S. Women's Open and the LPGA Championship four times each—a feat unmatched by any other female golfer. She was also the only person to win both titles in the same year twice, in 1958 and 1961.

Wright made it into the Pro Golf Hall of Fame in 1964, the same year she shot an 18-hole record score of 62 in tournament play. In 2001, Sweden's Annika Sorenstam became the first woman to shoot 59, equaling the men's record held by Al Geiberger, Chip Beck, and David Duval.

Can't Beat Koufax

Since he entered the National League in 1955, Sandy Koufax had proved to be a pretty good starter, but one who sometimes struggled with his control and who had not yet developed into a 20-game winner. In 1963, however, the Los Angeles Dodgers' left-hander put it all together for the first time in his nine seasons and developed into a dominating ace. Koufax had a 25–5 record that included 11 shutouts, a 1.88 earned run average (ERA, the number of runs charged to the pitcher times nine divided by the number of innings he pitched), 306 strikeouts, a no-hitter, the National League Most Valuable Player award, and the first of his three Cy Young Awards (when the award was given to just one pitcher from both leagues). Koufax was the first National League pitcher since 1939 to win pitching's unofficial Triple Crown by leading the league in wins, strikeouts, and ERA.

Football Shrine *The Pro Football Hall of Fame opened its doors in 1963. The first class inducted into the shrine in Canton, Ohio, included 17 former star players or significant contributors.*

1963

More importantly, Koufax helped the Dodgers sweep the mighty New York Yankees in the World Series in October—the first time the Yankees had gone winless in a Series since 1922. Koufax was nearly unhittable in the Series, pitching two complete games and allowing just three runs to win the Most Valuable Player award. He twice beat Yankees pitching ace Whitey Ford—in the opener and in the final game.

Mr. Hockey

Gordie Howe (b.1928) of the Detroit Red Wings surpassed Maurice Richard (1921–2000) as the all-time leading goal scorer in NHL history on November 10. Howe scored a short-handed goal (his team was short a player, due to a penalty) against Richard's old team, the Montreal Canadiens, for goal number 545 in his career.

Other Milestones of 1963

✔ The Boston Celtics won their fifth NBA title in a row, beating the Los Angeles Lakers in six games in the Finals. The Celtics were loaded, with stars such as Sam Jones (the team's leading scorer that year at 19.7 points per game), Tommy Heinsohn (18.9 points), Bill Russell (16.8 points and 23.6 rebounds), and John Havlicek (14.3 points). But the man who brought them all together was 34-year-old Bob Cousy (13.2 points in 1962–63). The best playmaking guard of his era, Cousy had already announced his retirement after 13 dazzling seasons. For his career, he averaged 18.4 points, 7.5 assists, and 5.2 rebounds per game.

Jesus, Matty, and Felipe Alou

✔ Jimmy Piersall was a one-of-a-kind baseball player. When he played outfield for the Boston Red Sox, he would bow after making easy catches. He'd also flap his arms like a seal. On June 23, Piersall, playing for the New York Mets, hit his 100th career home run. He celebrated by running around the bases backward!

✔ On September 15, the outfield was filled with Alous in a baseball game between the San Francisco Giants and the Pittsburgh Pirates. The Alou brothers—Felipe, Matty, and Jesus—all played together in the Giants' outfield for one inning. The Giants won the game, 13–5.

✔ With Ralph Baldwin in the sulky (a very light horse cart, designed for racing), Speedy Scot became only the second standard-bred horse in history to win the Triple Crown of trotting. In 1955, Scott Frost had been the winner of the Yonkers Futurity, the Hambletonian, and the Kentucky Futurity, the three legs of the Triple Crown for three-year-old trotters.

✔ The United States Gymnastics Federation, now called USA Gymnastics, was formed. It supports clinics, training camps, and team competitions, including programs to determine the U.S. National Team.

Howe was known as "Mr. Hockey," and with good reason. He retired holding nearly every NHL scoring record: most goals (801), most assists (1,049), most points scored (1,850), and most games played (1,767). His records seemed untouchable—that is, until Wayne Gretzky (b.1961) came along in the late-1970s.

Howe was big and strong, and he could skate and shoot. Once he planted himself in front of the net, he was tough to move. He led the league in scoring in four straight seasons, from 1950–51 to 1953–54. He won the Hart Trophy as the Most Valuable Player six times and played on the All-Star team 21 times.

Howe first retired in 1971. In 1973, the 45-year-old Howe came back to play with his sons, Mark and Marty, for the Houston Aeros in a new league, the World Hockey Association (WHA). The move was a public-relations natural for the WHA, which was badly in need of a star attraction in its uphill battle with the established NHL.

Howe played in the WHA until 1979, when the league merged with the NHL. By then, Howe had become a member of the Hartford Whalers. After the 1979–80 season, Howe called it quits for good. He was 52 years old and a grandfather. His combined NHL and WHA totals were 975 goals scored and 2,358 points during an amazing 32 seasons!

The Davis Cup

A Davis Cup meeting between men's teams from competing countries is known as a tie, and is a three-day event that consists of two singles matches on the first day, followed by one doubles match the next day, then two more singles matches on the final day. The tournament was started in 1900 by Dwight Davis, a tennis player from Harvard University, as a competition between the United States and Great Britain.

Davis Cup competition helped make tennis a popular international sport. In 1905, six countries competed for the Cup. By 1928, 33 countries were trying to win this trophy. The Davis Cup is the oldest trophy competed for by athletes around the world. (Hockey's Stanley Cup is seven years older, but is contested only by athletes who play for North American teams.)

U.S. Tennis Back on Top

At the Davis Cup tennis finals in Adelaide, Australia, the United States squad regained the international top spot, edging the four-time defending champion Australians, 3–2, to win the Davis Cup for the 19th time, but the first time since 1958. Chuck McKinley of Missouri outlasted Australian John Newcombe, 10–12, 6–2, 9–7, 6–2, for the decisive victory on December 29. As of 2002, the United States had won the Cup a record 31 times, followed by Australia with 20.

1964

Win One, Lose One

The San Diego Chargers played in two American Football League Championship Games in 1964. Well, two in the calendar year, that is, but in two different seasons. The first came on January 5 for the 1963 title. San Diego's Keith Lincoln rushed for 206 yards in a 51–10 rout of the Boston Patriots. Lincoln had a career day, also catching seven passes for 123 yards as the Chargers showed the nation how entertaining the passing offense of the AFL could be, by rolling up 601 total yards.

In the second game, to crown the 1964 champion on December 26, the Buffalo Bills beat the visiting Chargers, 20–7.

The Greatest

Cassius Clay (b.1942)—who soon would be known to the world as Muhammad Ali—was a brash, young upstart boxer. Sonny Liston was the fearsome, hard-punching heavyweight champion of the world. Liston was heavily favored when the two squared off in the ring on February 25 in Miami Beach, Florida. But it was Clay who emerged victorious with a technical knockout in the seventh round. And when it was over, Clay exclaimed over and over to anyone who would listen: "I am the greatest!"

Clay was born in Louisville, Kentucky. People called him "The Louisville Lip" because of the way he bragged. But he backed up his boasts in the boxing ring. He had a brilliant amateur career, highlighted by winning the light heavyweight gold medal at the 1960 Olympics. At 6-foot-3 and 215 pounds, Clay was big and strong, but he was also lightning fast, and he glided around the ring, taunting his opponents to hit him. After turning pro, Clay challenged Liston for the heavyweight title. Clay was the underdog, but he attracted attention by making up poems about what he would do to Liston in the ring. One of his handlers said Clay would "float like a butterfly, sting like a bee." He stung Liston enough to pull off a major upset victory in Miami.

Clay had been deeply interested in the Muslim religion, and after winning the title he became a Muslim and changed his name to Muhammad Ali. After nine title defenses, Ali was drafted into the U.S. military in 1967, during the Vietnam War. But he refused to go on the grounds that he was a Muslim minister (see page 69).

"I am the greatest!" *Boxer Muhammad Ali, then known as Cassius Clay, shouted after defeating Sonny Liston.*

He was sent to prison briefly, and boxing officials took away his title. In 1970, Ali was found not guilty of violating the draft law and allowed to box again. But his titles were not restored. He would have to get them back by winning in the ring.

In 1974, Ali knocked out the new champion, George Foreman (b.1948), and was again the heavyweight champ. He lost the title to Leon Spinks on February 15, 1978, but won it back against Spinks seven months later to become the first boxer to win the title three times. On November 9, 1996, Evander Holyfield beat Mike Tyson to join Ali as the only men to win the heavyweight title three times.

1964

The Barber of Michigan

At the Winter Olympic Games in Innsbruck, Austria, speed skater Terry McDermott from Michigan, a barber by profession, pulled off a major upset when he won the 500-meter speed skating gold medal on February 4. To make it even better, McDermott won on skates he borrowed from his coach! It would be the only gold medal for the United States in the 1964 Winter Games. The USSR dominated the Games, winning more than twice as many gold medals (11) and total medals (55) than any other country.

In preparation for his event, McDermott trained each afternoon at home by running and lifting weights. He also visited a hypnotist, who put the athlete in a trance and asked him what he needed to do to win the gold medal. When McDermott described the type of race he hoped to skate, the hypnotist told him, "For the next two years, you can skate that race every day and it will be in your subconscious so deep that when you skate in a big race, anywhere, it will be automatic."

This was very unorthodox at the time, but by the 1980s, it was not unheard of for athletes to seek the counsel of sports psychologists. By the 1990s, it was common for all pro sports teams to hire a person who specializes in enhancing athletic performance through mental imagery and other confidence-building techniques.

Beginning of a Dynasty

The University of California at Los Angeles won its first college basketball championship in 1964. UCLA did not lose a game all season. Its 30th, and final, victory of the season came in the NCAA title game on March 21, a 15-point thumping of Duke University, 98–83.

Five players started every game for UCLA: Keith Erickson, Gail Goodrich, Walt Hazzard, Jack Hirsch, and Walt Slaughter. The team was short on height—its tallest starter was 6-foot-5—but long on unselfishness. "This team came closer to realizing its full potential than any team I have ever seen," said coach John Wooden. The title was the first of 10 national championships in 12 years for UCLA.

South Africa Ban

South Africa sent athletes to the Winter Olympic Games for the first time in 1960 in Squaw Valley, California. Their participation proved short-lived, however. Before the 1964 Games, Olympic officials barred the nation from sending a delegation because of its segregationist policy, called apartheid, which deprived black South Africans of their civil rights. The ban was lifted in time for the 1994 Games, after apartheid ended.

Tough Way to Lose

It was a good news–bad news baseball game for pitcher Ken Johnson of the Houston Colt .45s (now the Astros) on April 26. The good news was that Johnson threw a no-hitter against the Cincinnati Reds. The bad news was that the Reds won the game, 1–0. Johnson became the first pitcher to throw a complete game no-hitter and lose! He gave up the winning run in the ninth inning after he and his second baseman made errors.

Hard luck was nothing new for Johnson, a right-hander whose lifetime record for seven teams was 91–106. "One game against the Phillies, they had a 'Runs for Johnson Night,' and any woman with a run in her stockings got in for free," he recalled of his Colt .45 days. "And then Jim Bunning beat us with a one-hitter."

Venturi's Last Stand

Ken Venturi kept his cool as temperatures soared toward 100 degrees during play at the U.S. Open Golf tournament at the Congressional Country Club in Washington, D.C. Venturi, a once-promising pro who hadn't won on the Professional Golfers' Association (PGA) Tour in four years, had lost his swing and his confidence. But he found it in the heat, firing rounds of 66 and 70 on the 36-hole final day, June 20. It was good enough to win the tournament by four strokes over runnerup Tommy Jacobs.

Venturi was close to heat exhaustion after his morning round. At the 16th tee, overcome by the scorching heat, he said to his playing partner, Raymond Floyd, "I don't know if I can make it in." He did, but he was accompanied by a doctor, who ordered Venturi to take rest periods, swallow salt tablets, and drink iced tea during the last 18 holes. In the final round, Venturi said, "The pin at the end of each hole looked like a telephone pole."

Phillies Phold

On September 21, ace right-hander Jim Bunning beat the Los Angeles Dodgers 3–2 to give the Philadelphia Phillies a six-and-a-half-game lead in the National League race with only 12 to play. Phillies' fans could be excused for excitedly looking ahead to the World Series. After all, they had played in the Fall Classic only two times and never won a championship in the 81-year history of the franchise. Could this finally be their year? Unfortunately . . . no.

The next day, Philadelphia dropped a 1–0 decision to the Cincinnati Reds, and the lead was down to five-and-a-half. The day after that it was four-and-a-half. Then three-and-a-half. In seven days, the Phillies lost seven games, and the lead was gone. Three more losses followed, running the losing streak to 10, and the St. Louis Cardinals, who pieced together an 11-game winning streak that overlapped Philadelphia's long losing streak, won the pennant. The "Phillie Phold" was the biggest late-season collapse ever.

St. Louis, which won on the final day of the season to clinch the pennant, went on to defeat the New York Yankees in seven games in the World Series in October (see page 43).

The disastrous ending overshadowed a terrific season for Bunning, a future Hall of Famer who won 224 games in his 17 big-league seasons. He won 19 games in 1964, one of them a perfect game in a 6–0 victory against the New York Mets on June 21 at Shea Stadium in New York. It was the first regular-season perfect game (no hits, no walks, no errors, no player reached first base) in 42 years. Bunning also became the first pitcher since 1900 to throw a no-hitter in both leagues (see the box on page 42).

Interleague Star

Jim Bunning could not have picked a better day for the highlight of his Major League Baseball career. Appropriately for a parent of seven children, Bunning's perfect game was on Father's Day. Needing only 86 pitches, Bunning pitched the first regular-season perfect game since Charlie Robertson of the Chicago White Sox did it in 1922. It was also the first perfect game in the National League since 1880. (In a perfect game, a pitcher allows no baserunners.)

Bunning was a two-league star. His first no-hitter came when he was on the American League's Detroit Tigers in 1958. He was traded to Philadelphia after the 1963 season. With his perfect game for the Phillies, Bunning joined a very exclusive group of pitchers who have had a no-hitter in both leagues. (Today, that group still has only four members: Bunning, Cy Young, Nolan Ryan, and Hideo Nomo.)

In those days, when a star player almost always stayed with one team for most of this career, Bunning was also the first modern-era pitcher to win 100 games in each league, the first to notch 1,000 strikeouts in each league, and the first to pitch in All-Star Games for both leagues.

Bunning retired after the 1971 season and later went into politics. He served in the Kentucky state legislature and was then elected to the U.S. Congress. He was elected to the Baseball Hall of Fame in 1996, and two years later to the U.S. Senate.

The Wright Stuff

Mickey Wright continued to be the dominant golfer on the women's tour and added another trophy to her case when she defeated Ruth Jessen in an 18-hole playoff to win the United States Women's Open at the San Diego (California) Country Club on July 12.

Wright shot a playoff-round 70 to earn a two-stroke victory over Jessen and equal the mark of four U.S. Open triumphs first attained by Betsy Rawls (b.1928). Wright previously won the Open in 1958, 1959, and 1961, while also earning a record four LPGA Championships during that time.

In all, Wright won 82 titles in her career to rank second on the all-time list behind Kathy Whitworth, who had 88 victories. Wright's 13 career wins in major tournaments is second to Patty Berg's 15.

In the Swim

Swimmer Don Schollander (b.1946) of Lake Oswego, Oregon, became the first swimmer to win four gold medals at one Olympic Games, and the first American to win four Olympic gold medals since Jesse Owens (1913–1980) in 1936. In the Games held in October in Tokyo, Japan, Schollander captured individual victories in the 100-meter freestyle and the 400-meter freestyle, and team wins by swimming the anchor legs of the 4-by-100-meter and 4-by-200-meter freestyle relays. He set world records in all events except for the 100—where he set an Olympic mark.

"This was the greatest moment in American swimming history," said U.S. swimming coach James Counsilman. Schollander, who was just 18, went on to win a gold medal and a silver medal at the 1968 Olympics in Mexico City.

Two-Sport Star

"Bullet" Bob Hayes, a 21-year-old speedster from Florida A&M University, was crowned the "World's Fastest Human" when he won the gold medal in the 100-meter dash at the Olympics. Hayes pulled away in the final 40 meters to bury the field, winning the race by seven feet—the widest margin of victory in Olympic history—while tying his own world record of 10 seconds flat.

Hayes later went on to become a pro football player and was the most successful of several speedy track stars who transitioned to wide receiver in the NFL. He was a three-time All-Pro receiver for the NFL's Dallas Cowboys and is the only man with an Olympic gold medal and a Super Bowl ring. In 2009, he posthumously was inducted into the Pro Football Hall of Fame.

Big Shot

Al Oerter (b.1936), a shot putter, won gold medals at the 1956, 1960, 1964, and 1968 Olympic Games, but his most amazing Olympic performance came in 1964. He suffered from extreme back pain, and less than one week before the Olympics he tore some rib cartilage (cartilage is elastic skeletal tissue). Doctors advised him to rest for six weeks, but Oerter decided to compete anyway. Before the shot-put event, Oerter told another athlete, "If I don't do it on the first throw, I won't be able to do it at all."

But Oerter's first throw only went 189 feet, 1 inch (57.63 meters). After four rounds, he was in third place. On his final throw, Oerter gave it his all. While he doubled over in pain, his discus sailed 200 feet, 1 inch (61 meters) to set another Olympic record and earn him a third gold medal. Oerter won his fourth gold in 1968. He was the first track-and-field Olympian to win his event four straight times.

End of a Dynasty

The National League-champion St. Louis Cardinals defeated the A.L.'s New York Yankees in October to win the World Series in seven games.

Good as Gold *That's American Olympic star Don Schollander on the far left in Tokyo in 1964. Fellow U.S. swimming gold medalists Gary Illman, Roy Saari, and Steve Clark pose with him.*

Other Milestones of 1964

✔ The American Football League received $36 million from NBC when the network agreed January 29 to televise its games for the next five years. The agreement gave each of the league's eight teams $900,000 a year to spend on players and operations. NBC's decision came after CBS won the right to broadcast NFL games for $28.2 million for two years.

✔ Bob Baun of the Toronto Maple Leafs was carried from the ice after fracturing his ankle while blocking a slap shot in game six of the NHL Stanley Cup finals against the Detroit Red Wings on April 23. In overtime, on the edge of elimination, Baun returned to the ice and scored the game-winning goal. Two days later, the Leafs won game seven with Baun still skating on a broken leg. It was Toronto's third Stanley Cup championship in a row.

✔ In November, St. Louis Hawks forward Bob Pettit (b.1932) became the first player in NBA history to score 20,000 points in his career. At season's end, Pettit retired with 20,880 points in 11 years. He averaged 26.4 points and 16.2 rebounds per game and twice was named the league's most valuable player.

✔ On August 1, Don Garlits (b.1932), the man fellow drag racers call "Big Daddy," was the first Top Fuel driver to surpass 200 miles per hour. Garlits drove his Swamp Rat dragster to victory in 35 National Hot Rod Association (NHRA) Top Fuel events in his career.

✔ The great thoroughbred Kelso (1957–1983) retired after winning his fifth consecutive Horse of the Year title. In 63 starts, Kelso won 39 races and finished second 12 times. He won nearly $2 million in his career—which was the most ever by a horse at the time. Such was America's love for this horse that he was sent letters and gifts from racing fans.

Don "Big Daddy" Garlits

✔ The first Wham-O Professional plastic flying disk, the Olympic Ring #1 model—soon to be better known as the Frisbee—rolled off the production line. By 1969, the Frisbee became such a part of American culture that astronauts took one to the moon.

✔ The batting glove was introduced by outfielder Ken Harrelson of the Kansas City Athletics. It's a thin, lightweight glove worn by the hitter to give him a better grip on the bat handle and to protect his hands from blisters.

The Yankees' Mickey Mantle, playing in his final Fall Classic, batted .333 with three home runs and eight runs batted in (RBI). His home run off St. Louis pitcher Barney Schultz in the bottom of the ninth inning to win game three gave Mantle 15 career World Series home runs, surpassing the mark set by Babe Ruth. Mantle played in 12 World Series and was on the winning team eight times. He holds World Series records for home runs (18), runs scored (42), RBI (40), walks (43), extra-base hits (26), and total bases (123).

The Cardinals prevailed in the 1964 Series, however, behind the overpowering pitching of Bob Gibson (b.1935), who won two Series games and struck out 31 Yankees in 27 innings.

The Series loss turned out to be an omen for the great Yankees' dynasty that started in the 1920s and peaked from 1947 to 1964. During those 18 seasons, the Yankees won 15 A.L. pennants and 10 World Series. But after never having to wait more than four years to reach a World Series, the Bronx Bombers did not make it back again for 12 years.

It was truly the end of an era. Dan Topping sold the Yankees to the CBS television network in 1964. The next year, the team, which had gone 40 years without a losing record, dropped to sixth place, and in 1966 finished dead last.

Wrong-Way Run

The first inkling that Minnesota Vikings defensive end Jim Marshall had that something was wrong came when he turned around in the end zone and a San Francisco player came up to congratulate him. Marshall had scored two points on a safety—for the 49ers!

In the third quarter of a game at Minnesota on October 25, a 49ers' player fumbled. Marshall scooped up the loose ball and started running toward the end zone. His teammates began yelling at him. Marshall thought they were cheering him on. Defensive players rarely touch the ball, much less score touchdowns. But in all the excitement, Marshall had gotten confused. He cruised 66 yards into the end zone—the wrong way!

When he returned home after the game, Marshall received hundreds of telephone calls from supportive friends.

"I still feel embarrassed about that play, and I suppose I'll never be allowed to forget it," says Marshall, who played in four Super Bowls and set an NFL record (since broken) by playing in 282 consecutive games. "But I don't see any reason to hide, either. If people want to laugh, I'll go along with it. At the time, I was hustling or the thing couldn't have happened."

And besides, the story does have a happy ending: Minnesota still won the game, 27–22.

Cleveland Rocks

Jim Brown of the Cleveland Browns, playing in his eighth pro season, became the first runner in NFL history to gain 10,000 yards in his career. Brown led the league in rushing for the seventh time in 1964, and he was a marked man in the NFL Championship Game against the Baltimore Colts. Cleveland kept Baltimore off balance with passing, but Brown still rushed for 114 yards on 27 carries to help the Browns win the title with a decisive 27–0 blowout at Cleveland's Municipal Stadium on December 27.

This was the last NFL title won by the original Cleveland Browns franchise. In 1996, team owner Art Modell moved the team to Baltimore, where the franchise changed its name to the Ravens. The Ravens won Super Bowl XXXV to conclude the 2000 season, and Cleveland was left without a pro football team until 1999, when NFL expansion plans brought a new team to the city and restored the Browns' name and uniforms.

1965

Big Man on Campus

Bill Bradley (b.1943) was named college basketball's Player of the Year after he led Princeton University all the way to the Final Four of the NCAA tournament. The senior scored a tournament-record 58 points to lead his team to a 118–82 rout of Wichita State, good enough for third place in the March tournament. Playing in the final game of his college career, Bradley was everywhere on the court. He sank 22 of 29 shots from the floor and 14 of 15 from the free-throw line, grabbed 17 rebounds, and dished out four assists. (Princeton had beaten Penn State, North Carolina State, and Providence to reach the Final Four before losing to Michigan in the semifinals.)

After college, Bradley studied as a Rhodes Scholar at Oxford University in England. In 1967, he joined the New York Knicks. Bradley went on to play 10 seasons in New York, where he helped the Knicks win NBA titles in 1970 and 1973.

After retiring from basketball, Bradley went on to even bigger accomplishments. He was a United States senator from New Jersey, and he ran for President of the United States in 1992.

Dome Sweet Dome

Baseball's Houston Astros became the first professional sports team to play its home games in a domed stadium, the Astrodome. The Astrodome was also the first stadium to have a field covered with plastic grass called AstroTurf.

The Astrodome, dubbed the Eighth Wonder of the World, opened in April to 47,876 curious fans, including the President of the United States, Lyndon Johnson, all of whom had come to watch an exhibition game between the Astros and the New York Yankees. Mickey Mantle got the park's first hit and its first home run. As if the dome wasn't enough, gimmicks included a scoreboard pyrotechnic display after each Astros' home run.

The original playing surface actually was a natural grass field, but the synthetic turf was installed in 1966 when the grass could not sustain its growth.

Nicklaus Rising

Jack Nicklaus took charge of the PGA Masters with a third-round 64 at Augusta National Golf Club in Augusta, Georgia, in April. Nicklaus shot a final-

Schoolboy Star *Lew Alcindor (33) went from a high school star to a college basketball powerhouse (page 48).*

round 69 to finish with a 17-under-par 271, the lowest total in Masters' history until Tiger Woods came along.

Nicklaus' nine-stroke victory over Arnold Palmer and Gary Player was the largest margin of victory in the 29-year history of the tournament, and was met with cheers, as the once-unpopular player was beginning to be recognized by the galleries for his greatness.

"Havlicek Stole the Ball!"

The scene was the Boston Garden, April 15, game seven of the Eastern Division NBA finals. The Philadelphia

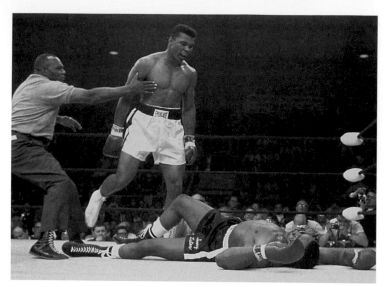

Quick Work *Heavyweight champion Muhammad Ali (standing) needed less than two minutes to retain his crown against Sonny Liston in a rematch of their 1964 title fight.*

76ers trailed the Boston Celtics, 110–109, with five seconds remaining in the game. The 76ers still had a chance. Philadelphia's guard, Hal Greer, attempted to pass the ball inbounds to Chet Walker, but Boston's John Havlicek (b.1940) leaped and tipped the ball to teammate Sam Jones (b.1933). The raspy radio call by Celtics announcer Johnny Most—"Havlicek stole the ball! Havlicek stole the ball!"—became one of the most famous sports broadcasts of all time.

In the championship round, the Celtics defeated the Los Angeles Lakers—who were led by Wilt Chamberlain, the league's leading scorer—in five games to capture their seventh straight title.

A Gentle Giant

Lew Alcindor (b.1947) was one of the most talked-about players to come out of New York City. As a 6-foot-8 teen-

ager, he led Power Memorial High School to a record of 95 wins and only six losses. He won All-America honors his last three years and led the school to three city championships. On May 4, Alcindor, the first basketball player to be highly recruited on a national level, announced his decision to accept a scholarship to play for coach John Wooden at UCLA.

In three varsity seasons, Alcindor's teams won 88 games and lost only two. A two-time player of the year, he led UCLA to three national titles and was named the NCAA tournament MVP all three times. UCLA won back-to-back championships in 1964 and 1965, and could now claim true dynasty status with five national titles in six years. Alcindor, who had grown to 7-foot-1, was such an unstoppable scorer that, in 1967, the NCAA outlawed dunking to slow him down. (The dunk was legalized again nine years later.)

Alcindor was the first player picked in the 1969 NBA draft, by the last-place Milwaukee Bucks. In the 1970–71 season, he averaged 31.7 points per game and teamed with Oscar Robertson to lead the Bucks to an NBA title. During the season, he changed his name to Kareem Abdul-Jabbar. He had been a Muslim since college, and he wanted to show his faith publicly. Abdul-Jabbar won six MVP awards and was a member of six NBA championship teams. In his 20-year career, he set many league records, including most points scored (38,387).

The Phantom Punch

 Muhammad Ali retained the heavyweight championship when he

knocked out Sonny Liston in the first round of their rematch in Lewiston, Maine on May 25. Ringside officials scored the KO at one minute, the media at 1:42, and referee Jersey Joe Walcott at 2:17.

No matter whose clock you time it by, the fight was still over in round one. No other heavyweight title bout was decided that early until Mike Tyson dispatched Michael Spinks in 91 seconds in 1988.

The quick ending was controversial, and some spectators yelled "Fake!" and "Fix!" Many were angered because the punch—a short right hand that sent the 215-pound Liston to the canvas for the first time in his career—did not seem to have knockout power. The press would sarcastically label the final blow "The Phantom Punch." The 204-pound Ali called it his anchor punch, and when he delivered it to his opponent's head, Liston dropped like an anchor, lying on his back as Ali stood over him shouting, "Get up and fight, sucker!"

Gatorade Hits the Spot

In the early 1960s, a team of researchers at the University of Florida began developing a drink that could replace lost body fluids and help prevent dehydration in athletes. In 1965, the drink was tested on the school's football players. The drink became known as Gatorade after the University of Florida Gators.

The special lemon-lime drink paid immediate dividends. Gators who sipped Gatorade during the 1966 season reported fewer problems with dehydration and seemed to have better endurance. The football team won eight of 10 games and triumphed in the 1967 Orange Bowl against the number-one ranked and undefeated Georgia Tech squad, 27–12. When *Sports Illustrated* asked coach Bobby Dodd why his team lost, Dodd said, "We didn't have Gatorade." Coaches across the country soon began to buy Gatorade, hoping to give their team an edge.

Football Expansion Wars

War between the professional football leagues started off the 1960s with a bang. The upstart American Football League set up new teams in Boston, Denver, Houston, Oakland, and Buffalo. Then they established clubs in New York, Los Angeles, and Dallas to compete with existing NFL teams. Its first year, 1960, the AFL adopted a 14-game schedule for its eight teams. The next year the NFL increased its schedule to 14, too.

The Gatorade Dump

Former New York Giants linebacker Harry Carson and defensive lineman Jim Burt started the tradition of dumping Gatorade on winning coaches. The first wet victory celebration to gain national attention took place in 1987, when the Giants won the Super Bowl.

Carson was superstitious. For good luck, he drenched Parcells after each win during the 1986 season. Carson and Burt sneaked up on coach Bill Parcells and showered him with Gatorade. "It was really Jim's idea," said Carson. "But I helped pull it off on Parcells the first time." It really did turn out to be a good-luck charm: The Giants won 17 of 19 games, including the Super Bowl.

What did it feel like to be drenched from head to toe with Gatorade? "Cold!" says Parcells. "But it felt good, too, because it meant we had won."

1965

By 1965, the AFL and NFL were staging expansion wars, as both leagues raced to place clubs in new cities. The NFL had already awarded franchises to Dallas and Minneapolis-St. Paul, and grew to 13 teams. On June 3, the NFL decided to expand from 14 to 16 teams. Four days later, the AFL expanded from eight to 10 teams for 1966, and to 12 teams by 1968.

The two leagues carried on a fierce bidding war for players, driving the price of football talent sky high. The battle began with the AFL's first player draft in 1959. The AFL had wealthy owners in its favor as it went up against the 40-year-old NFL. With its big bucks and growing reputation for quality football, the AFL attracted many superior players. But its biggest prize was Joe Namath (b.1943). In 1965, the AFL's New York Jets signed the popular and talented Alabama quarterback for an unheard-of $427,000 contract, the biggest salary ever given to an athlete. The money signaled that the AFL was here to stay, and within a year, both leagues agreed to a merger (see page 58).

Swinging a Dangerous Bat

Juan Marichal (b.1937), who was born in the Dominican Republic, was the most successful Latin American pitcher in history and the second Latino player elected to the Baseball Hall of Fame, after Roberto Clemente (1934–1972). Unfortunately, Marichal is often best remembered for an incident that took place on August 22, at Candlestick Park in San Francisco. Marichal and the San Francisco Giants were playing their in-state rivals, the Los Angeles Dodgers.

The Dodgers and Giants were longtime foes, and both teams were battling against one another for the National League pennant, so tensions were running high. Early in the game, Marichal had hit two Dodgers with pitches. When it was Marichal's turn at bat, the ball brushed Marichal's ear as Dodgers catcher John Roseboro threw it back to pitcher Sandy Koufax. Marichal hit Roseboro on the head with his bat, giving the catcher a deep gash and a concussion. A nasty brawl followed. Marichal was suspended for eight days and slapped with the biggest fine ($1,750) in National League history at the time. Marichal apologized and always regretted the ugly incident.

From 1962–1971, Marichal was one of the dominant pitchers in the National League, averaging 20 wins per season. Ironically, Roseboro campaigned for Marichal's election to the Hall of Fame after the pitcher was passed over in his first two years of eligibility. In Marichal's induction speech in 1983, delivered in both English and Spanish, he offered special thanks to Roseboro.

Koufax the Magnificent

Los Angeles Dodgers left-hander Sandy Koufax became the first pitcher to throw four no-hitters in his career. On September 9 against the Chicago Cubs, Koufax struck out 14 and retired all 27 batters he faced for a perfect game!

Poor Bob Hendley, the Cubs' pitcher, only gave up one hit in his team's 1-0 loss. Nolan Ryan (b.1947) broke Koufax's record with his fifth no-hitter in 1981.

In 1965, Koufax put up some of the best numbers of any pitcher ever, going 26–8, with eight shutouts, an N.L.-leading 2.04 ERA, and a major league-record 382 strikeouts (until Ryan broke that record, too, in 1973). Then the southpaw from Brooklyn dominated the Minnesota Twins by pitching shutouts in games five and seven of the World Series to lead Los Angeles to victory. He wrapped up his season by winning the Cy Young Award.

Unveil the Hype Machine

As more and viewers turned on a television set to get their sports, team owners worried about the effect on attendance. To keep the turnstiles spinning with people coming out to the ballpark, teams for the first time used creative promotional techniques. The hapless Kansas City Athletics staged two memorable marketing gimmicks in an effort to lure fans into buying tickets.

On September 8, Bert Campaneris became the first player in modern baseball history to play all nine defensive positions in one game. Campaneris, usually a shortstop, played a different position in each inning. Later that season, at the age of 59, Satchel Paige (1906–1982), the greatest pitcher in the history of the Negro Leagues, pitched three innings for Kansas City and became the oldest player

Bond of Brothers

Gale Sayers's right knee buckled from a tackle in the ninth game of the 1968 season. He had immediate surgery to repair massive ligament damage. After undergoing a difficult rehabilitation program, Sayers returned in 1969 to finish first in the NFL in rushing for the second time, with 1,032 yards. That marked the first time a running back had gained more than 1,000 yards in a season after knee surgery.

Sayers showed immense courage and determination in getting back into playing condition. For that achievement, Sayers was awarded the Comeback Player of the Year. When he received the award, he was thankful, but said he would give the trophy to his teammate, Brian Piccolo. Piccolo, Sayers's close friend and roommate during road trips, had helped him during his difficult rehab programs. Now, Piccolo was in a battle with cancer. He died a few weeks later.

As roommates, Sayers, who is African-American, and Piccolo, who was white, had to overcome their own racial prejudices, as well as those of their teammates. Their friendship was immortalized in Sayers's book, *I Am Third*, which was made into a television movie, *Brian's Song*, starring Billy Dee Williams as Gale Sayers and James Caan as Brian Piccolo. In 1971, *Brian's Song* aired on ABC. It won five Emmy Awards.

1965

ever to play in a major-league game. Age seemed irrelevant to Paige, who once said, "Don't look back, something might be gaining on you."

The First Spike

The first spike of a football in an NFL game took place on October 17. The innovator was New York Giants receiver Homer Jones. It happened in the second quarter of a game against the Philadelphia Eagles. Jones scored on an 89-yard pass from Earl Morrall.

It was Jones's first NFL touchdown, and he wanted to celebrate in a big way. Jones was about to throw the ball into the cheering crowd—but the NFL fined players for throwing the ball into the stands. "That would have cost me $500," says Jones. "So I threw the ball down as hard as I could."

Soon other players started copying Jones's celebration spike. Today, almost all touchdowns are punctuated by this scoring celebration—and more!

Six Times Six

Chicago Bears' rookie running back Gale Sayers (b.1943) burst into the National Football League record book on December 12 when he scored six touchdowns in his team's 61–20 rout of the San Francisco 49ers at Wrigley Field. Sayers equaled the record first set in 1929 by the Chicago Cardinals' Ernie Nevers and matched in 1951 by Dub Jones of the Cleveland Browns.

Sayers had 113 yards rushing, 89 yards receiving, and 134 yards returning kicks against the 49ers. His combined total of 336 yards still ranked as the seventh highest of all time nearly 40 years later. (Sayers also ranked sixth with 339 combined yards in a game played on December 18, 1966.)

Sayers was nicknamed "The Kansas Comet." After playing college football at the University of Kansas, he joined the Bears in 1965. In just his third game, he scored four touchdowns. Not surprisingly, Sayers was named the NFL's Rookie of the Year. He combined for 2,272 yards, scored more touchdowns in a season (22)

The Kansas Comet *Rookie Gale Sayers burst onto the scene for the Chicago Bears in 1965. Sayers was a silky smooth runner the likes of which the NFL has not seen since.*

Other Milestones of 1965

✔ In the NCAA basketball championship on March 20, UCLA guard Gail Goodrich scored a title-game record 42 points (later surpassed by Kentucky's Jack Givens in 1978) to lead the Bruins to a 91–80 win over Michigan and their second straight championship. The UCLA dynasty was off and running.

✔ The Montreal Canadiens won their record 11th Stanley Cup hockey championship in May, defeating the Chicago Blackhawks in seven games.

✔ In motor sports, race car driver Jim Clark surpassed 150 miles per hour at the Indianapolis 500 on May 31 and ushered in the era of rear-engine cars.

✔ Cincinnati Reds pitcher Jim Maloney no-hit the New York Mets for 10 innings June 14 before losing the game 1–0 on a home run in the 11th. But two months later, on August 19, Maloney no-hit the Chicago Cubs for 10 innings. This time, he was a 1–0 winner when teammate Leo Cardenas homered in the top of the 10th.

Gail Goodrich

than anyone before him, and scored the most points ever by a rookie (132). He led the league in scoring in 1965 and was runnerup in rushing, punt returns, and kickoff returns.

Sayers went on to lead the NFL in rushing in 1966 and 1969. He averaged five yards per carry and a record 30.6 yards per kick return for his career. Unfortunately, knee injuries forced him to retire after just seven seasons. His was among the shortest and sweetest careers in pro football history.

At 34 years old in 1977, he was the youngest player to be inducted into the Pro Football Hall of Fame.

From Bills to Laws

Pete Gogolak kicked three field goals and the Buffalo Bills' smothering defense did the rest as the Bills blanked the San Diego Chargers, 23–0, on the road to win their second straight American Football League title on December 26. Jack Kemp, the future Congressman from New York and a vice-presidential candidate in 1996, quarterbacked the Bills to the AFL championship in 1964 and 1965. The Bills made it to the 1966 AFL title game, but lost, 31–7, to Kansas City.

1966

Bigger and Better

For more than two decades, despite the sport's increasing popularity, the National Hockey League declined to expand beyond its six teams: the Boston Bruins, New York Rangers, Chicago Blackhawks, Detroit Red Wings, Montreal Canadiens, and Toronto Maple Leafs. On February 9, however, NHL owners decided that the time was right. They voted to allow six new teams—all based in the United States—to begin play in the 1967–68 season. The new franchises were the Los Angeles Kings, Minnesota North Stars, Philadelphia Flyers, Pittsburgh Penguins, Buffalo Sabres, and St. Louis Blues. (The Blues reached the Stanley Cup finals in their first season.)

Expansion changed the face of pro hockey. From 1942 to 1967, nearly all the players were from Canada, and few Americans outside of the northern parts of the United States cared much about hockey. However, much has changed over the past 40-plus years. The NHL now has 30 teams. American players have become stars. So have top players from countries all over the world, such as Sweden, Finland, the Czech Republic, and Russia.

New Era in Labor Relations

Few men who never played Major League Baseball have had such an impact on the sport as did Marvin Miller (b. 1917), who spent 17 years as executive director of the Major League Baseball Players' Association beginning in March of 1966. The former chief of the tough steelworkers' union brought that steely reserve to baseball labor relations, and his experience overmatched the team owners, whom he routinely outwitted. Miller changed the fortunes of baseball players and, by extension, all athletes, forever. By the time he retired in 1983, the average salary had skyrocketed from $19,000 to $240,000. Today, that figure is well over $2 million.

Among Miller's other miracles was an end to the reserve clause, which bound a player to his team even when his contract was up. The reserve clause had always been a part of Major League Baseball, and was upheld in 1922 by the Supreme Court as part of the game's antitrust exemption. Free agency, under which a player can freely negotiate with any team when his contract is up, resulted in much higher salaries. Miller also introduced labor disputes, the right of veteran players to veto

Dynamic Duo *Right-hander Don Drysdale (left) and left-hander Sandy Koufax (right) were a formidable pair, both on the field and in labor negotiations (see page 57).*

1966

trades, a vastly improved pension plan funded largely through percentages of television revenue, and recognition of the players' union, which led to the right to collective bargaining.

Miller may have been as unpopular with some fans as he was with the owners, because he led two player strikes—a 13-day strike at the beginning of the 1972 season and a 50-day walkout in the middle of 1981—but his tough tactics finally got the players a bigger piece of the pie in a time of baseball prosperity.

The Golden Jet *Chicago Blackhawks wing man Bobby Hull possessed a combination that was lethal to opponents: He was the fastest man in hockey and had one of the most powerful slapshots.*

Golden Jet Takes Flight

Blond-haired Bobby Hull (b.1939) was so fast a skater that he became known as the "Golden Jet." The superstar left wing of the Chicago Blackhawks dominated the National Hockey League during the 1960s with his spectacular playing style, breaking scoring records and bringing an excitement to the game that rarely had been seen before.

Hull was electrifying as he glided across the ice at nearly 30 miles an hour—faster than any other man in his sport. His slap shot, which intimidated opposing goaltenders with its accuracy and speed, was once clocked at 118 miles an hour! Hull's straight-on shot became even scarier when he and teammate Stan Mikita (b.1940) began experimenting with different ways of curving their stick blades. The best method seemed to be heating the wooden blade with a propane torch, which made the wood slightly flexible, and then shaping the curve of the blade by hand to achieve the desired effect. With just the right curve, when Hull unleashed his slap shot, the rock-hard rubber puck was on the rise as it careened toward the goalie.

Goalies had bad dreams the night before facing Hull's wicked slapper. No wonder other goalies followed Jacque Plante's lead, and by 1966 almost all of them were wearing a hard plastic mask to protect their face.

On March 12, in a game against the New York Rangers at Madison Square Garden, Hull became the first NHL player to score more than 50 goals in a season. He scored his 51st goal in the season's

Powerful Pair

If baseball players needed an example of the power of collective bargaining (see page 54), they needed only to look to Los Angeles, where star pitchers Sandy Koufax and Don Drysdale (1936–1993)—who had teamed to help the Dodgers win the World Series for the second time in three years the previous fall—staged a join holdout that rocked baseball shortly before the start of the 1966 season.

Koufax and Drysdale demanded that Dodgers owner Walter O'Malley pay them $1 million over three years, to split evenly between them, or $167,000 each for the next three seasons. They threatened to leave the game if their demands were not met. They also insisted that the Dodgers deal with their lawyer, not with them. Though common today, dealing with someone who was acting as a player's agent was unheard of then. The two pitchers had led the Dodgers to world championships in 1963 and 1965 and felt they had a right to be treated as "coequal parties to a contract."

O'Malley refused to negotiate, and in the end both sides could claim something of a victory. Eventually, Koufax got $125,000 and Drysdale got $110,000. The two pitchers became the highest-paid players in the game while also setting a bargaining example for their fellow major leaguers.

61st game. Hull's record goal came on a 40-foot slap shot at 5:34 of the final period, tying the game at 2–2. The Blackhawks, who went on to win, 4–2, had set up a screen in front of Cesar Maniago, the Rangers' goalie, when Hull shot.

Hull, a 27-year-old, 5-foot-10, 195-pounder, won his second consecutive Art Ross Trophy as the league's Most Valuable Player in 1965–66. He finished his record-setting season with 54 goals and 97 points. Other players, including Hull, had scored exactly 50 in a season, but nobody had ever done that twice, so Hull was also the first player to score 50 goals in a season more than once. And he was the player with the highest single-season point total to date. Before Hull's career ended, he reached the 50-goal mark three more times, for a total of five 50-goal seasons.

In 1972, Hull stunned the NHL by taking a better deal with the upstart World Hockey Association. He signed a 10-year contract for a whopping $2.75 million, including an additional $1 million signing bonus. The WHA owners needed Hull's star drawing power for the league to survive. Thanks to the effort of Hull and another former NHL superstar, Gordie Howe (b.1928), the WHA lasted seven seasons.

Landmark Hoops Game

Texas Western College, with an all-black starting five, outplayed all-white University of Kentucky in the game that would be called the *Brown vs. Board of Education* of college basketball. (The famous Supreme Court ruling in *Brown* outlawed school segregation across the United States.) The Texas Miners (whose school eventually changed its name to the University of Texas–El Paso) defeated the Kentucky Wildcats 72–65 on March 19 to win the NCAA men's basketball title.

1966

Although both teams entered the final game with 26-1 records, legendary Kentucky coach Adolph Rupp (1901–1977) had said, "No five blacks are going to beat Kentucky." Rupp, age 64, had won four national championships as coach of Kentucky, and he had never allowed a black player on his team. But on Texas Western's second possession, David Lattin sent a clear message to Kentucky when he slammed a vicious dunk over a stunned Pat Riley, the Wildcats' star player (and later a championship-winning NBA coach). Then with 10 minutes gone in the first half, the smallest man on the court, Bobby Joe Hill (1943–2002), stole the ball on consecutive Kentucky possessions and

Basketball Breakthrough *Texas Western's all-black team shocked Kentucky to win the college title.*

converted both steals into layups. From there, Texas Western dominated much of the rest of the game.

The game made a lasting impression on many sports fans because this was an era when few important teams started more than two or three black players. Don Haskins (1930–2002), the coach of Texas Western, said the game's historic significance didn't sink in until he received "bushelsful of hate mail." Years later, when asked if he regretted that the race issue overshadowed his team's accomplishments, Haskins said, "All I did was play my best people. It was that simple" (as quoted in his December 13, 2002, obituary in *The New York Times*).

In 1969, Rupp recruited his first black player, then he retired. More than 40 years later, the Miners' victory is still hailed as the signature moment for the racial integration of college sports.

Pro Football Makes Peace

A series of clandestine meetings between American Football League representative Lamar Hunt (the owner of the Kansas City Chiefs) and National Football League representative Tex Schramm (the general manager of the Dallas Cowboys) led to a merger between the two pro-football leagues on June 8. It ended seven years of war between the leagues.

The merger agreement called for the first combined draft in 1967, with the idea of eliminating costly bidding wars. The merger was not going to be fully in place until 1970, when the two leagues' multimillion dollar television contracts ended. But the next step, after the com-

A Transforming Legacy

After Bill Russell (b.1934) started playing in the National Basketball Association, the pro game was never the same. The 6-foot-9 center changed basketball by showing how a player could dominate a game by playing spectacular defense. No one had ever done that before. During the 13 seasons he played for the Boston Celtics, they won 11 NBA titles!

Russell was the first player to take over a game without necessarily scoring much. For a long time, teams tried to win games by sinking as many baskets as possible. But Russell showed that defense and rebounding could win games, too. In a typical game, Russell grabbed at least 20 rebounds. He once had 51 rebounds in a single game! In all, he grabbed 21,620 rebounds, for an average of 22.5 per game. Only Wilt Chamberlain (1936–1999) has more career rebounds.

Russell was a great shot-blocker, too. He had long arms and he studied the shooting routines of other players. When an opponent took a shot, Russell was there to block it. He once told an opponent to bring salt and pepper to a game, because he was going to make him eat basketballs! Russell didn't try to swat the ball out of bounds. Instead, he looked to gain control of the ball or tap it over to a teammate to start the Celtics off on a fast break and an easy basket.

Russell was a winner everywhere he went. At the University of San Francisco, his team won 55 straight games between 1954 and 1956. They won back-to-back NCAA titles in 1955 and 1956. Russell was the tournament's most outstanding player in 1955. After winning a gold medal as a member of the 1956 Olympic basketball team, Russell was drafted by the Celtics. He led Boston to the NBA championship in his first season. They were also champs in every year from 1959 through 1966—eight seasons in a row! Red Auerbach, the Celtics' longtime coach, said, "Bill put a whole new sound in pro basketball—the sound of his footsteps."

In 1966, Russell took over as the player-coach of the Celtics and became the first African-American to coach a major-league professional team in any sport. In 1968 and 1969, Russell guided the Celtics to two more NBA championships. He later served as general manager and coach of the Seattle SuperSonics and as head coach of the Sacramento Kings.

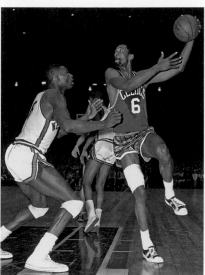

Bill Russell

bined draft, was a world championship game pitting the two champions from each league against one another—the first Super Bowl (see page 64).

Ironically, the bitter feud between the AFL and NFL eventually resulted in a healthier professional football league. Because of competition between the two leagues, the AFL awarded franchises to cities where NFL teams were already established, and the NFL raced to place clubs in new territories, making football

1966

a truly national sport. With television investing in both the NFL and AFL, each team's television revenues grew as more fans turned on their TV sets. Players' salaries were growing higher, but so were the number of fans filling the stadiums.

Cloninger's Grand Day

Atlanta Braves right-hander Tony Cloninger had a dream day against the San Francisco Giants on July 3. Not only did he toss a complete game in the Braves' 17–3 rout at Candlestick Park, but he also drove in nine of his team's runs! It was the most ever by a pitcher.

Atlanta was ahead 3–0 in the first inning when Cloninger connected for a grand-slam home run off the Giants' Bob Priddy. It was 9–0 in the fifth when he did it again: a grand slam off Ray Sadecki. For good measure, he added a run-scoring single off Sadecki in the eighth inning.

Cloninger was a decent hitter for a pitcher, but his nine RBI were more than he had in any other season in his career.

The Art of Compromise

In order to bring about the NFL-AFL merger, NFL commissioner Pete Rozelle (1926–1996) negotiated some strange compromises. One of them concerned which ball to use for the first league championship game. The Wilson Sporting Goods Company made the official ball of the NFL. The AFL used a Spalding ball. Since the shapes of these balls were slightly different, both leagues wanted to use their own ball. A compromise was arranged. During the first NFL-AFL World Championship Game, a Wilson ball had to be used when the NFL team played offense. When the AFL team played offense, the ball was a Spalding.

Baltimore Is for the Birds

Outfielder Frank Robinson (b.1935) of the Baltimore Orioles was named the American League's Most Valuable Player. Robinson, who had won the MVP award with the Cincinnati Reds in 1961, became the first baseball player to win the award in both leagues.

In his first season with the Orioles, Robinson won the Triple Crown—topping the league in batting average (.316), home runs (49), and runs batted in (122)—and in October, the imposing outfielder led his team to a sweep of the Los Angeles Dodgers in the World Series.

Robinson was named MVP of a 1966 World Series dominated by pitchers. That year, the Dodgers and the Orioles played in the lowest-scoring World Series in history. Both teams had great pitching staffs. The Orioles had Jim Palmer (b.1945), who would be a Hall of Famer, and the Dodgers had Sandy Koufax and Don Drysdale, who also were future Hall of Famers. Yet the star of the series was Robinson. He hit .286 with a triple, two homers, and three runs batted in. That may not sound like a lot, but Robinson's three RBI were more runs than the Dodgers scored in the whole series! Robinson hit a home run in the final game, giving the Orioles a 1-0 win and their first world championship.

When a Tie Equals Victory

Notre Dame coach Ara Parseghian had to know that the jokes soon would be coming—and they did. The Fighting Irish soon were derisively called the "Tying Irish" by their critics. The famous saying was no longer, "Win One for the Gipper," it was "Tie One for the Gipper." But Parseghian knew what he was doing when his top-ranked team settled for a 10–10 tie with No. 2 Michigan State in college football's biggest game of the season on November 19. The game was played in front of 80,011 frenzied fans at Michigan's Spartan Stadium and another 30 million watching at home—the largest television audience ever for a regularly scheduled college football game.

The much-ballyhooed matchup became a crisis for Notre Dame midway in the first quarter, when starting quarterback Terry Hanratty (b.1948) got knocked out of the game by a shoulder separation when Bubba Smith (b.1945), the Spartans' 283-pound lineman, fell on top of him. The Irish led the nation in scoring offense under the leadership of Hanratty, who passed for 1,247 yards on the season. But without its quarterback, Notre Dame's offense was forced to play conservatively. Still, despite its impressive offense, defense had been the key to the success of this Notre Dame team, which shut out six of its last eight opponents.

Parseghian (b.1923) compiled a record of 95–17–4 during his 11 seasons at Notre Dame beginning in 1964, and deserves credit for returning the team to its past glory. But he will forever be accused of lacking courage in the Michigan State game after he chose to run out the clock and settle for a tie to preserve his team's national ranking. The Irish had their shot at victory, but Parseghian ordered four running plays after getting the ball for the last time on his own 35-yard line with a minute and a half to play. "If it was

early in the fourth quarter it would have been different," said Parseghian, "but we weren't going to give up the ball deep in our territory and take a risk of losing the game after battling like we did."

The strategy worked, as both Notre Dame and Michigan State finished the season with identical 9–0–1 records. But the Irish were named the number- one team in the polls.

Out on Top

Lots of pro athletes like to say that it's their dream to walk away from sports at the height of their glory, with their talents undiminshed by age or injury. But for whatever reason—whether it's the lure of bigger and bigger paychecks, the adulation of the fans, or simply the unquenchable desire to compete —few men (or women) who make their living playing sports retire in their prime. Pro Football Hall of Fame member Jim Brown is the exception to the rule. In 1966, Brown, considered by many observers to be the greatest fullback ever, retired from football to pursue an acting career.

At the time, Brown was only 30 years old and was coming off a season in which he had won the league's Most Valuable Player award. In nine seasons with the Cleveland Browns, from 1957 to 1965, Brown never missed a game or a Pro Bowl. By the time he retired, he held just about every rushing record imaginable, including a career mark of 12,312 rushing yards—or almost seven miles! He also scored 126 touchdowns.

Brown set his amazing number of records when the NFL season was only 12

1966

and then 14 games long. Today's players are trying to break those same records under the current 16-game schedule. No matter. More than 40 years after his retirement, Brown still holds four league records. He led the NFL in rushing for eight of his nine professional seasons, which is unmatched in NFL history. His career average of 5.22 yards per carry is the best ever by a running back.

Brown was nearly unstoppable when he was running with a football. It took at least two people to tackle Brown, if they could catch him. Even then, the 6-foot-2,228-pound bruiser often dragged his defenders right over the goal line. He ran over tacklers if he couldn't get around them. He never ran out-of-bounds to avoid a hit. "Make sure when anyone tackles you he always remembers how much it hurt," Brown once told tight John Mackey, another Hall of Famer.

What was the best way to tackle Brown? Said former New York Giants linebacker Sam Huff, a Hall of Famer, "Grab hold, hang on, and wait for help."

Besides his acting career (he appeared in *The Dirty Dozen* and *100 Rifles*, among other films), Brown has worked to help African-Americans improve their economic situation. Along with being an outspoken critic of unfairness and racism, he also works to rehabilitate gang members in the Los Angeles area. He was elected to the Pro Football Hall of Fame in 1971.

What Matters Most

Sandy Koufax grew up in Brooklyn, New York, in a Jewish family. He took his heritage seriously, and refused to pitch when games were played on the holiest of Jewish holidays, Rosh Hashanah and Yom Kippur—which always came in the fall. In fact, the Dodgers took the Jewish High Holidays into consideration when setting their pitching rotation, so that Koufax could pitch as much as possible during the pennant race in late September and the World Series in early October.

In October 1965, Koufax's principles were tested when the Dodgers and Minnesota Twins met in the World Series. The opening game fell on Yom Kippur, holiest day of the Jewish year, and Koufax was not at the ball park. Don Drysdale pitched in his place and the Dodgers lost 8–2. The next day, the *St. Paul Pioneer Press* published a sports column titled, "An Open Letter to Sandy Koufax." It contained a number of distasteful jokes and references to Jewish customs. The column ended, "The Twins love matzah balls." (Pitches that are hit for home runs are usually called "meatballs.")

Later, Koufax remarked, "I couldn't believe it. I thought that kind of thing went out with dialect comics." He pitched the second game in the Series and lost 5–1. But he won the seventh and deciding game, and the Dodgers won the World Series. After that, Koufax said, "I clipped the column so that I could send it back to him [the writer of the column] after we defeated the Twins, with a friendly little notation that I hoped his words were as easy to eat as my matzah balls. I didn't send it. We were winners."

Other Milestones of 1966

✔ Nineteen years after Jackie Robinson broke baseball's color barrier, the Opening Day crowd at Washington's Griffith Stadium on April 11 watched as Emmett Ashford, baseball's first African-American umpire, took the field. Major League Baseball's first black manager, Frank Robinson, wasn't named until 1975.

✔ Tennis player Billie Jean King, at age 22, won her first major tournament, the Wimbledon singles final, after stunning the defending champion, Margaret Court, in a straight-set semifinal match on July 2.

Emmett Ashford

✔ Nineteen-year-old Jim Ryun set a new world record in the mile run with a time of 3 minutes, 51.3 seconds during a competition at Edwards Stadium in Berkeley, California. Ryun's sizzling time shaved a remarkable 2.3 seconds off the previous record, set in 1965 by Michel Jazy of France.

✔ On September 13, Baltimore Colts quarterback John Unitas surpassed Y.A. Tittle to become pro football's all-time leader for most touchdown passes. Six weeks later, Unitas broke Tittle's mark for the most passing yards.

Koufax KO'd by Injury

Like Jim Brown, Los Angeles Dodgers ace left-hander Sandy Koufax still was at the top of his game when he retired on November 18. Unlike Brown, though, the 30-year-old Koufax's decision was made for him, in large part, because of injury. "I am leaving the game while I can still comb my hair," he said.

Koufax was the National League's Cy Young Award winner as the top pitcher for the second consecutive season in 1966. Also for the second year in a row, he topped the league in wins (27), ERA (1.73), innings pitched (323), and strikeouts (317). But he suffered from severe arthritis in his throwing arm, which caused him incredible pain. Sometimes he lost all feeling in his pitching hand. His arm swelled enormously after each game and had to be iced. He had to take countless cortisone shots, and didn't want to risk permanent damage to his left arm—or his health.

Between 1962 and 1966, Koufax was the game's most dominating pitcher. He won three Cy Young Awards—when the award was given to just one pitcher from both leagues—and was the National League's Most Valuable Player in 1963. In addition, he pitched four no-hitters, including a perfect game. He helped the Dodgers win four pennants and three World Series. In 1972, at the age of 36, he became the youngest man ever elected to the National Baseball Hall of Fame.

1967

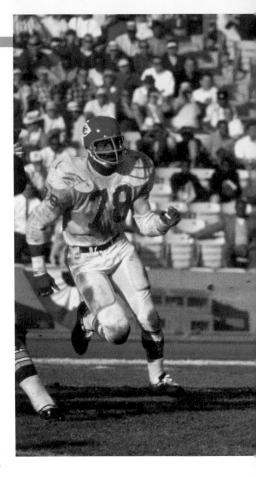

The First Super Bowl

Little did anyone realize the enormity to which the Super Bowl would grow when the Green Bay Packers defeated the Kansas City Chiefs 35–10 in the first game between the champions of the National and American Football Leagues, held in Los Angeles on January 15.

That first Super Bowl wasn't even called the Super Bowl back then. Officially, it was called the "AFL-NFL World Championship Game." There were lots of other differences between the game then and now, too.

For instance, only 63,036 fans attended the game at the Los Angeles Memorial Coliseum. That meant more than 30,000 seats were empty. (There is no such thing as an empty seat at a Super Bowl these days.) Many of the spectators left by the fourth quarter.

The game was broadcast on two television networks. An estimated 60 million curious viewers tuned in to watch either on NBC or CBS. At least twice that many people watch the Super Bowl today.

And a ticket to the first Super Bowl cost $12. The cost of a ticket to Super Bowl XLIV, in January 2010, was $325.

Bart Starr (b.1934), the quarterback of the NFL's Packers, was the MVP of Super Bowl I. He completed 16 of 23 passes for 250 yards and two touchdowns. Both of the touchdowns went to Max McGee, a 34-year-old substitute who was in action only because starting receiver Boyd Dowler got hurt early in the game. McGee's first touchdown came on an outstanding one-handed catch of a pass thrown behind him. McGee, who caught only four passes during the regular season, had 7 receptions for 138 yards against the Chiefs.

Starr was at his best in postseason games. In two Super Bowl appearances, he completed 29 of 47 passes for a total of 452 yards.

Powerful Pack *Green Bay running back Donny Anderson follows the blocking of guard Gale Gillingham.*

The Packers dominated the NFL during the 1960s—nine players from the Packers of the 1960s have been elected to the Pro Football Hall of Fame—and victory in the first Super Bowl cemented their dynasty. Yet this was a pressure-packed game for the players. They had just won their second straight NFL title and their fourth in six years. Now the Packers were representing the entire NFL and would be embarrassed to lose to a team from a seven-year-old league.

The veteran Packers knew they were in a challenging game against the upstart Chiefs, and led only 14–10 at halftime.

Doubt about the outcome disappeared in the third quarter, when Green Bay stretched its lead to 28–10. The key play came on the fourth play after halftime. That's when all-pro safety Willie Wood intercepted a pass and returned it 50 yards deep into Chiefs' territory.

The NFL was relieved to have captured bragging rights in the first Super Bowl game. At the time, there was real hatred between the leagues. But in three years, the leagues merged, and so the animosity of one league versus another soon died. The spectacle of the Super Bowl, however, got bigger and bigger.

How the Super Bowl Got Its Name

The first two Super Bowl games were called the AFL-NFL World Championship Game. That terrible tongue-twister was NFL commissioner Pete Rozelle's idea. "I guess coming up with catchy names wasn't something I was very good at," said Rozelle.

Lamar Hunt, the owner of the Kansas City Chiefs of the AFL, got the idea to name the game the Super Bowl from his children's favorite toy: the Super Ball. "I was just kidding at first when I mentioned the Super Bowl in meetings," said Hunt. "But then the other owners starting using it and the press started picking it up."

Rozelle didn't like the name, saying, "To me, 'super' was a corny, cliché word." Thankfully, Hunt convinced the other team owners to adopt the name. The term "Super Bowl" became official in 1969 with Super Bowl III.

The use of Roman numerals actually began with Super Bowl V, which was won by the Baltimore Colts over the Dallas Cowboys 16-13 on Jim O'Brien's 32-yard field goal with five seconds remaining. The Roman numerals were adopted to clear up any confusion that might occur because the Super Bowl is played in January of the year following a season.

New Kid on the Block

While the upstart AFL and the established NFL were making peace, a war between the new American Basketball Association and the established National Basketball Association was just beginning. The ABA began play in 1967. It had 10 teams. The league lasted only nine seasons, but it made important contributions to professional basketball. It featured an All-Star Slam-Dunk Contest, and it introduced the three-point shot more than a decade before the NBA.

ABA Commissioner George Mikan (1924–2005) instituted a red, white, and blue ball for league play. Critics suggested that the ball looked as if it had bounced off the nose of a seal. But the league had many stars, most notably Julius Erving (b.1950), known as "Dr. J." Erving was the ABA's Most Valuable Player in the league's last three seasons (he shared the 1975 award with George McGinnis).

The league went out of business in 1976, but four of its teams—the Denver Nuggets, Indiana Pacers, New York (now New Jersey) Nets, and San Antonio Spurs—were invited to join the NBA. As of the 2002–03 season, the Spurs are the only former ABA team to win an NBA championship (they'd done it twice).

A New League's First Star

Rick Barry, a senior at the University of Miami, led the nation in scoring during the 1964–65 college basketball season. The following year he was NBA Rookie of the Year with the San Francisco (now Golden State) Warriors. In 1966–67, the year he led the NBA in scoring with 35.6 points per game, Barry almost single-handedly took the Warriors to the championship. The team lost to the Philadelphia 76ers, but Barry was outstanding in the April series, averaging 40.8 points per game—a record that lasted until Michael Jordan broke it in 1993.

In 1967, the new American Basketball Association needed big-name stars to attract fans. In June, Barry became the first NBA star to jump to the new league when he signed with the Oakland Oaks after the franchise hired University of Miami basketball coach Bruce Hall—Barry's father-in-law—as head coach. But Barry had legal troubles before he ever stepped onto an ABA court. In August, a court ruled that his contract obligated him to play one more year for the Warriors. Barry decided to sit out the season instead. When he finally played again in 1968–69, he averaged 34 points a game for the Oaks—the highest average in the league. Barry is the only player to have led the NCAA, NBA, and ABA in scoring.

In 1972–73, Barry went back to the NBA to play for the Warriors. Sinking his famous underhand free throw again and again, Barry led the league in free throw percentage for the first of four times in his career. He had his best season in 1974–75, when he scored 30.6 points per game, was sixth in the NBA in assists (with 6.2 per game), and led the league in steals. Most important, he helped the under-rated Warriors win their only league title since the team moved from Philadelphia to the West Coast. The Warriors swept the Washington Bullets in four games in May. Barry capped his great season by averaging 28.2 points per game in the playoffs and winning the Finals MVP Award.

No Dunking Allowed

UCLA, led by its new star, Lew Alcindor (who eventually changed his name to Kareem Abdul-Jabbar), forged another perfect season (30–0) in college basketball. In the NCAA championship game, Alcindor scored 20 points and grabbed 18 rebounds in a 79–64 rout of the University of Dayton on March 25. It was UCLA's third NCAA title in four years, with the promise of more to follow. Alcindor—just a sophomore—averaged 29 points and already dominated the college game like nobody before him.

Opposing coaches felt they needed to cut Alcindor and UCLA down to size. And his almost unstoppable slam dunk seemed a good place to start. Basketball traditionalists found the dunk boring to watch, and critics said the stuff shot gave an unfair advantage to the new breed of taller players. After the 1966–67 season,

Bay Bridge *The Warriors' Rick Barry led the NBA in scoring in 1966–67 before bolting across the Bay Area to Oakland.*

67

1967

the National Basketball Committee of the United States and Canada (a body of college coaches) banned all dunking and stuffing. The group's stated reasons: There is no defense against the dunk, and that upsets the balance of the game; players can injure themselves; dunking breaks backboards and bends basket rims.

In reality, the Alcindor Rule, as it came to be called, was a sorry attempt by the coaching fraternity to keep UCLA from winning another national title. It was one year since an all-black Texas Western team defeated an all-white Kentucky team for the national title (see page 57), and race relations were on shaky ground. Many people saw more than coincidence in the fact that the dunk was outlawed just when Alcindor, who is black, began to dominate the college game. Others considered the rule the last desperate act of racially insensitive "basketball purists," frustrated at watching the game become an increasingly high-wire game dominated by talented African Americans.

Did the no-dunk rule work? Well, in Alcindor's two remaining college seasons, UCLA lost just two games and won two more national titles. The rule forced Alcindor to perfect his jump shot and develop a different shot that was virtually impossible to defend against—the "sky hook" (a hook shot in which he held the ball high over his head).

Dunking eventually was made legal again in 1976. During a game that year, an overly excited Wiley Peck of Mississippi State dunked so hard that the ball came through the net and hit him in the face, knocking him cold for two minutes.

Run for Glory

Four miles into the Boston Marathon on April 19, photographers taking pictures from a flat-bed truck noticed a woman in the race. At the time, major races such as the Boston Marathon were open only to men. Track officials believed that a woman's body was not able to endure the stresses of running for 26.2 miles.

A couple of race directors were on a bus following the photographers, and one of the directors, Jack Semple, hopped out and tried to remove the woman, Kathy Switzer, from the race. Several male runners, who long had realized Switzer was a woman, tried to shield her from the official. Then Switzer's 235-pound boyfriend leveled Semple with a cross-body block, and Kathy kept on running. She didn't stop until she had completed the marathon in an unofficial four hours, 20 minutes.

Switzer had obtained a number to compete when race officials accepted an entry form from K.V. Switzer of Syracuse University. The incident was much publicized. Pictures of the race official trying to tear the number off Switzer's jersey were seen around the world. In 1972, women were finally made an official part of the race that is held annually on Patriot's Day in Boston.

Although Switzer was not the first woman to complete the Boston Marathon (Roberta Gibb was an unofficial participant in 1966), she did pave the way for a future generation of female runners. Finally, in 1984, the Olympics allowed women to compete in the marathon. Joan

Benoit of the United States won the first Olympic marathon gold medal at the Los Angeles Summer Games on August 5.

Ali Takes a Stand

"I ain't got no quarrel with those Vietcong." With that famous statement to reporters, boxing champ Muhammad Ali articulated the feelings of many Americans who were against the controversial, ongoing war in Vietnam.

By 1967, the Vietnam War had been raging for almost eight years. U.S. military involvement in the conflict had grown considerably in that time, while at home anti-war feelings had grown even more rapidly. Millions of Americans objected strongly to American troops being sent to Southeast Asia to fight against Communist Vietcong rebels. In addition, a high percentage of the soldiers were African American, and the ongoing Civil Rights Movement added this to their list of grievances against the government and its treatment of black citizens.

In the middle of this, Ali got a letter that changed his life and, in many ways, the ongoing relationship between sports and politics.

At that time, the U.S. government held an annual draft to fill the ranks of the armed forces. Young men were assigned a draft number based on their birthday, and when their number came up, they were required by law to report for duty. Ali was aware of this, and for months, had been trying to have himself classified as a "conscientious objector" (CO). COs are people who object to war or violence because of religious beliefs. Ali felt that his beliefs

Muhammad Ali, CO *After refusing to step forward when called to the draft board, Muhammad Ali (left) was arrested and led out of the Lexington, Kentucky Army facility.*

in Islam, specifically his membership in the American Black Muslim movement (which he had joined in 1964, see page 38), prohibited him from fighting in a war. However, the government did not want Ali to become a symbol of Black Muslim power and refused to make him a CO. The fateful letter told him that he had been drafted, and, on April 28, Ali reported to the draft board in Louisville to join the

Vietnam War

In the late 1950s and early 1960s, the United States became involved in a civil war in the nation of Vietnam in Southeast Asia. Communist-backed rebels from the north of the country were battling Western-backed forces in the South. Over the course of the decade, several hundred thousand American soldiers spent time in the conflict, which became known as the Vietnam War.

The war bitterly divided the United States as it went on, with many protestors calling for an end to U.S. involvement. The "anti-war" movement was greatly inspired by boxer Muhammad Ali's refusal to fight. He became an important symbol of resistance.

The U.S. left Vietnam for good in 1975. The country today is unified under a government that remains after the forces from the north won the conflict.

Army. In a scene that would become a noted historical moment of the 1960s, an Army sergeant called out, "Cassius Marcellus Clay, step forward." Ali refused. By refusing, Ali was committing a federal crime, evading the draft.

Reaction was swift and harsh. In June, Ali was convicted after a trial of draft evasion, sentenced to five years in prison, and fined $10,000. As the case was appealed, his passport was taken away, so he could not travel. Then, Ali was stripped of his heavyweight title by international boxing authorities. Over the next few years, however, many things would change, in America and in the world, and Ali would rise to the top again. By 1971, he was back in the ring. By 1975, the war was over.

Looking back, Ali still believes he made the right choice. In the 1991 book, *Muhammad Ali: His Life and Times*, by Thomas Hauser, Ali said, "Standing up for my religion made me happy. It wasn't a sacrifice. When people got drafted and sent to Vietnam and didn't understand

what the killing was about and came home with one leg and couldn't get jobs, that was a sacrifice. But I believed in what I was doing, so no matter what the government did to me, it wasn't a loss."

Engines Move to the Back

On May 31, A.J. Foyt won the Indianapolis 500 auto race for the third time in seven years. Foyt's first two triumphs, in 1961 and 1964, were in front-mounted, Offenhauser-powered roadsters. This time, the 32-year-old Texan had a Ford engine in the rear end of a Coyote chassis, a racer of his own design.

The 1960s was an important decade for motor sports technology. In 1963, a funny looking racing car appeared on the Indy 500 track. It was light, a bit flimsy looking, and it had an engine at the wrong end—the rear end! Folks laughed at first, but with the great Scottish driver Jim Clark behind the wheel, maybe there was something to this new technology. And while Parnelli Jones eventually won the 1963 race driving his front-engine Offenhauser, the "Flying Scot" was not far behind in his rear-engine spidery critter.

The rear-engine machine quickly became the racing car of the future. By 1964, 12 of the 33 Indy 500 entrants drove rear-engine machines. By 1966, only one front-engine racer qualified to start the race.

The King

Richard Petty (b.1937) won more races than anyone else in NASCAR history—and it's not even close. Petty took the checkered flag 200 times in his storied racing career. The No. 2 driver on the all-time list, David Pearson, won 105 times. Petty won the prestigious Daytona 500 seven times—that's a record—and won seven season championships—another record, since tied. (Drivers receive points for the order in which they finish. The driver with the most points at season's end wins the title.) It's little wonder that Petty's nickname is "The King."

In 1967, Petty streaked through the most dominant season in NASCAR history. He set a record by winning 27 races, including 10 in a row, out of 48 starts in 1967. He also won his 55th career race, passing his father, Lee, for the most ever.

The King retired in 1992. Now his son Kyle is a driver on the circuit, giving the Petty family three generations of successful stock-car racers.

The Impossible Dream

In 1966, the Boston Red Sox finished in ninth place in baseball's 10-team American League. And when the 1967 season began, Boston fans had no reason to believe their team would improve much. But under the guidance of new manager Dick Williams, and behind the 22 wins from pitcher Jim Lonborg, the Red Sox turned things around. In the closest race in A.L. history, four teams, including the Red Sox, were still battling it out in the last week of the season.

Boston's leftfielder, Carl Yastrzemski (b.1939), almost singlehandedly lifted the Red Sox to the pennant. Boston needed to win the last two games of the regular season against the Minnesota Twins to avoid a three-way tie with the Twins and

the Detroit Tigers. "Yaz" had seven hits in eight at-bats, with five runs batted in, to lead the Red Sox to two victories and their first pennant in 21 years.

Yastrzemski won the A.L. Most Valuable Player award for 1967, as well as the Triple Crown, leading the league with his .326 average, 44 home runs, and 121 runs batted in. He continued his hot hitting in the World Series in October, batting .400

Long Live the King *Stock-car racer Richard Petty won an amazing 27 races in 1967. He retired a quarter-century later with a record 200 victories—more than double his closest competitor.*

1967

in the Fall Classic against the St. Louis Cardinals. But in the Series, St. Louis pitcher Bob Gibson (b.1935), who won three games, and the Cardinals were too much for the Red Sox, who lost in seven games. Boston's Fenway faithful called the 1967 season "the impossible dream."

O.J.! Oh My!

The rivalry between the University of Southern California Trojans and the UCLA Bruins is one of the fiercest in all of college football. On November 18, the two crosstown rivals met in a game at the Los Angeles Coliseum that had much at stake. On the line was a Rose Bowl bid, a possible national championship, and, perhaps, the Heisman Trophy.

UCLA came into the game undefeated and ranked number one in the nation. Led by their senior quarterback, Gary Beban, the Bruins broke a 14–14 tie early in the fourth quarter when Beban threw his second touchdown pass of the game. But USC's Bill Hayhoe blocked Zenon

Other Milestones of 1967

Billie Jean King

✔ Bobby Orr of the Boston Bruins won the Calder Memorial Trophy as hockey's best rookie player. Three years later, he became the first defenseman to lead the league in scoring. That 1969–70 season was Orr's coming-out party. He became the first hockey player to win four individual season trophies: the regular-season Most Valuable Player, league scoring leader, outstanding defenseman, and playoff MVP.

✔ Billie Jean King won the women's titles at Wimbledon and at the U.S. Open. King also teamed with Rosemary Casals and Australian Owen Davidson to win the women's doubles and mixed doubles at both Wimbledon and the U.S. Open, making her the first woman to accomplish that sweep since Alice Marble in 1939.

✔ Bowling continued to gain in popularity, and bowling alleys continued to introduce new innovations. In the 1960s, bowling proprietors helped patrons who could not figure out the sport's unique scoring method. Bowling alleys introduced the new automatic score.

✔ In December, the United States Soccer Association and the National Professional Soccer League combined to form the 17-team North American Soccer League (NASL). The NASL, which eventually attracted several big-name world stars, lasted through 1984.

Andrusyshyn's extra-point try, leaving the score 20–14. The missed conversion was critical, because USC had a star of its own, magnificent halfback O.J. Simpson (b.1947), who rushed for 177 yards and two scores. Simpson ran for the winning touchdown only moments later. It came on a dazzling 64-yard run that began with Simpson taking a handoff, faking right, and then sprinting around the left end of the field. He cut toward the middle of the field at the Bruins' 40-yard line and, sprung by a block from Earl McCullouch, outran his pursuers into the end zone. The extra point was good, giving USC a hard-fought 21–20 victory.

The Trojans went on to defeat Indiana University 14–3 in the Rose Bowl in Pasadena, California, in January. Coach John McKay's USC team finished the season with a 10-1 record and captured the national championship. Simpson rushed for 1,415 yards in 266 attempts during the season, averaging 5.3 yards per carry and scoring 23 touchdowns. But the UCLA quarterback, Beban, won the Heisman Trophy in a close race. Simpson won the award the following year as a senior.

The Ice Bowl

The Green Bay Packers and Dallas Cowboys closed the calendar year in 1967 by playing one of the most famous games in NFL history on December 31. Quarterback Bart Starr ran one yard for the winning touchdown in the closing seconds of a 21–17 victory that gave the Packers the NFL championship. The dramatic title game has come to be known as the "Ice Bowl." The temperature on the field was measured at minus-13 degrees Fahrenheit, but the frozen tundra of Green Bay's Lambeau Field made it feel like 35 below zero with the wind chill.

The Packers trailed the Cowboys 17–14 with 16 seconds left in the game, but Green Bay had the ball on the Dallas one-yard line. It was third down, and the Packers called their last time out. Coach Vince Lombardi could choose a safe pass into the end zone; if it failed, he could kick an easy field goal for the tie. If he chose to run, the Packers had enough time for only one play. On the sidelines, quarterback Bart Starr suggested a quarterback sneak (where the quarterback fakes handing off the ball, but actually runs with it himself). Lombardi agreed. In the huddle, Starr called a play for a handoff to a running back, who would plow over Packer right guard Jerry Kramer into the end zone. Only Lombardi and Starr knew the quarterback would actually keep the ball.

On a playing field frozen rock hard, Kramer dug his foot into an unusually soft area of turf and made a critical block against a bigger opponent, Cowboys defensive tackle Jethro Pugh, which allowed Starr to score the winning touchdown, giving the Packers a 21–17 victory. Green Bay won its third straight NFL title and advanced to Super Bowl II against the Oakland Raiders. The Packers beat Oakland in January 1968 to win their second straight Super Bowl (see page 74).

1968

Packers Are NFL Top Dogs

When it was over, the Green Bay Packers players carried head coach Vince Lombardi off on their shoulders. "The best way to leave a football field," Lombardi once called it.

Lombardi's team had just defeated the Oakland Raiders 33–14 in Super Bowl II at the Orange Bowl in Miami, Florida on January 14. It was the Packers' second straight victory in the Super Bowl and the last game on the sidelines for Lombardi, who had recently announced that he would step down as coach to become a front-office executive.

Lombardi symbolized America's obsession with professional football in the 1960s. From 1960 to 1967, he coached the Packers to six conference titles, five NFL championships, and victories in Super Bowls I and II. No other coach in NFL history has a better winning percentage. In his 10-year coaching career, his teams won nearly 75 percent of their games! To honor his dedication to winning, the NFL renamed the Super Bowl trophy the Vince Lombardi Trophy.

Lombardi worked his players until they were near exhaustion, making the games seem easy by comparison. He stressed the team concept and punished any player who was late for practice. Players set their watches ahead 10 minutes to what they called "Lombardi time." The coach was tough, but he was fair. "He treats us all the same," said defensive tackle Henry Jordan. "Like dogs."

Building a Champion

In 1959, when Vince Lombardi took over as coach of the Green Bay Packers, the team was coming off its worst record in history (1–10–1). He had inherited an awful team. But he began molding the squad in his own vision. He promoted third-stringer Bart Starr to starting quarterback, appointed reserve fullback Jim Taylor the starting position, and switched backup quarterback Paul Hornung to full-time running back. All three players became Hall of Famers.

But Lombardi's greatest achievement was shaping a championship team from the rubble. In 1961, when the Packers won their first of five titles in seven years, 14 of the 22 starters were players who had been with Green Bay in that awful 1958 season.

Hockey Helmet Law

Bill Masterson of the Minnesota North Stars died from a brain injury after hitting his head on the ice during a

Power Pitcher   *The St. Louis Cardinals' Bob Gibson (throwing, above) was baseball's best pitcher in 1968, but the Detroit Tigers' Mickey Lolich led his team to victory in the World Series.*

hockey game with the Oakland Seals on January 15. The 29-year-old center was the first player in the 51-year history of the National Hockey League to die from a game-related injury. He was not wearing a helmet. This prompted league discussion about making helmets mandatory, but the NHL did not pass a helmet rule until the 1979–80 season. Even then, it only required players who joined the league after that point to wear a helmet.

When Craig MacTavish retired following the 1996–97 season, he entered the history book as the last player to play in the NHL without a helmet. MacTavish played for 17 seasons in the NHL and was instrumental in helping his teams win four Stanley Cups; three with the Edmonton Oilers and one with the New York Rangers. In June 2000, MacTavish was named the Oilers' coach.

Battle of the Big Men

 The game between the University of Houston Cougars and the UCLA

1968

Bruins at the Astrodome on January 20 was one of the epic matchups in college basketball history. It pitted the Cougars' 48-game home winning streak against the Bruins' 47-game winning streak, the second longest in college basketball history; Houston center Elvin Hayes (b.1945) against UCLA big man Lew Alcindor; and the No. 1 team in the nation (UCLA) against No. 2.

In the end, the hometown Cougars won 71–69 before 52,693 fans in attendance and a national television audience. Hayes' two free throws with 28 seconds to play—to shouts of "E! E! E!"—made the difference.

The 6-foot-8 Hayes, known as "The Big E," scored 39 points, grabbed 15 rebounds, and blocked four shots. He also contained the 7-foot-1 Alcindor, a junior who scored only 15 points, but was playing with a scratched eyeball that had caused him to miss UCLA's two previous games.

Two months later, the Cougars brought a 32-game winning streak into the NCAA tournament, and the two teams faced off again in a much-anticipated semifinal game. This time, the Bruins turned the tables. Alcindor had 19 points and 18 rebounds while limiting Hayes to 10 points in a 101–69 UCLA rout on March 22. The next day, Alcindor scored 34 points in the final as the Bruins beat North Carolina 78–55. It was UCLA's fourth championship in five years under coach John Wooden.

The Ice Queen

The United States won only one gold medal at the Winter Olympic Games in Grenoble, France, in February, but it was a memorable one by figure skater Peggy Fleming (b.1948). Her triumph helped change the face of international skating.

Fleming was a graceful skater who made tough moves look easy. She won the U.S. figure skating championship and the hearts of Americans in 1964, when she was just 15 years old. She went on to win five national titles, three world titles, and the Olympic gold medal.

Fleming's victory in the Olympics was not only a personal triumph, but also a victory of the ballet approach over the athletic approach to figure skating.

Golden Girl *Adding a light, dance-like touch to her athletic skating maneuvers, American Peggy Fleming cruised to an Olympic gold medal at the Winter Olympics in Grenoble, France.*

Until the graceful Colorado State College skater came along, women's figure skating threatened to be dominated by skaters who stressed athletic jumping ability. But Fleming, at 5-foot-4 and weighing only 108 pounds, represented a more dance-like approach in which the elements blend smoothly as the skater flows across the ice.

Events at the 1968 Winter Games foreshadowed the struggles between the International Olympic Committee (IOC) and the athletes. The first hint of the brewing storm occurred when the president of the IOC, Avery Brundage (1887–1975), threatened to cancel the skiing events unless athletes removed the manufacturers' labels on their equipment. Although he temporarily backed away from this rigid position, he had laid the foundation for a more explosive incident in the next Olympics. Austrian skier Karl Schranz was banned three days before the 1972 Olympics opened for accepting payments from his equipment manufacturer.

Derby Disqualification

Dancer's Image crossed the finish line one and a half lengths before the runner-up horse, but was not the official winner of the Kentucky Derby at Churchill Downs in Lexington, Kentucky on May 7. Dancer's Image was disqualified after a post-race drug test revealed traces of an illegal substance used to reduce swelling. Forward Pass was declared the winner, and Dancer's Image was destined to remain the only Kentucky Derby winner ever disqualified.

Tennis' Open Era

Before 1968, tennis players had to be amateurs to compete in tournaments such as Wimbledon and the U.S. Open. That meant that they earned no prize money. As a result, some of the best tennis players were leaving the amateur ranks, and were not playing in the major tournaments. In 1968, when officials at the Wimbledon tournament in England realized that their event was going to be held without the world's best players, they decided to allow both pros and amateurs to compete in Wimbledon.

As soon as Wimbledon offered prize money, almost all the other tournaments did as well. That began the open era of tennis, with major events open to both amateurs and pros.

The first U.S. Open of the new era in tennis pitted tennis professionals against amateurs. The 1968 men's title went to an amateur, Arthur Ashe (1943–1993), who defeated Tom Okker of Holland in a marathon five-set final, 14–12, 5–7, 6–3, 3–6, 6–3. Ashe received $15 a day in expense money; Okker, a professional, pocketed the $14,000 winner's check.

Ashe was the first African-American tennis player to win the men's singles title at the U.S. Open and at Wimbledon—which he won in 1975 as a professional. During his pro career, Ashe won 51 tournaments and often represented the U.S. as a member of the Davis Cup team, which competes against other countries. In 1979, Ashe had a heart attack and was forced to retire. After his career, he became well known for his views on racial equality and justice. During a heart operation, he

Controversial Book—
Controversial Subject

The black athlete was a visible symbol of America's attempt for equality between the races. The breakthrough that Jackie Robinson made by busting through baseball's color barrier in 1947 was extending to other sports. If a black athlete in basketball or football was superior to a white teammate, it was logical that the black player would be in the starting lineup. That's the equal nature of sports: the player who can run faster and jump higher and score more points will play, regardless of skin color.

During the early part of the decade, the black athlete was considered to be a posterboy of racial progress: teamed alongside white counterparts and cheered by millions of white fans. But that colorblind image merely scratched the surface. Underneath was a black view of sport to which the majority of white Americans were blind. Jack Olsen opened eyes with the publication of his groundbreaking 1968 book, *The Black Athlete: A Shameful Story*, on the brewing issue of race and sports. The book sparked nationwide debate when it was excerpted in a five-part series published by *Sports Illustrated* in the summer of 1968.

"The world of professional sport offered great opportunity to the Negro," wrote Olsen, "but it did not offer him equality." Brewer's book said that black athletes needed more talent than white athletes to be in the starting lineup, and second-stringers were almost exclusively white athletes. Black players were paid less money than whites of comparable ability, and certain positions on the field that required intelligence, judgment, authority, and responsibility were almost automatically "white only." In football, for instance, "thinking" positions like quarterback were virtually banned to Negroes. In baseball, few African-Americans were represented on the pitchers' mound.

After years of battling for fair opportunities, people of color are finally making inroads. Professional sports team's rosters are filled with African-Americans, and although the number of black coaches, managers, and executives is still a small percentage, the ranks are swelling. Today, there's a new generation of African-Americans, Latinos, Asians, and Native Americans who have risen to positions of power on and off the playing field.

became infected with HIV, the virus that causes AIDS. He died in 1993.

Politics at the Olympics

Throughout history, the Olympic Games have reflected the times in which they are played. The 1960s were an emotionally charged decade. The struggle over human rights and the Vietnam War, in particular, resulted in assassinations, civil-rights protests, and anti-war rallies.

The spirit of the 60s was also reflected at the 1968 Summer Olympics in Mexico City, held in October.

The Games saw a burst of record-breaking performances in the track-and-field events, perhaps helped along by the thin air of high-altitude Mexico City. The games were also rocked by protest over racial injustice. American sprinters Tommie Smith and John Carlos caused a sensation on the victory platform after the 200-meter dash by bowing their heads and raising gloved fists during the playing of the U.S. National Anthem. Their purpose was to publicize and protest prejudice against blacks in sport and society. Avery Brundage, the IOC president, was furious over the silent, non-violent protest and expelled both athletes from the Olympic village.

Beamon Takes Flight

Waiting his turn in the finals of the Summer Olympics long-jump competition in Mexico City in 1968, American Bob Beamon had no inkling what was coming. "Don't foul. Don't foul," he said to himself. That doesn't sound like the exhortation of a man who was about to jump farther than any other man in history.

Beamon not only didn't foul, but he soared nearly six feet into the air, landing with a world-record jump of 29 feet 2.5 inches (8.9 meters). The world mark, which had increased only 8.25 inches since 1935, had just been shattered by an astonishing 21.75 inches—nearly two feet!

Beamon's leap has been called the greatest single athletic achievement of all time. But he almost never got the chance to compete for the gold medal. Beamon grew up in South Jamaica, New York, and attended the University of Texas at El Paso. In 1968, there was a great deal of racial turmoil in the United States as African Americans marched and protested to obtain equal rights. In April of that year, six months before the Olympics, Beamon was suspended from his college track team after he refused to compete against Brigham Young University, because he felt the school had racist admission policies. As a result of his suspension, he had to train for the Olympics without a coach.

In Mexico City, Beamon was in trouble in the qualifying round. He stepped over the takeoff line and fouled on his first two attempts. He was one foul away from being eliminated. Before his third jump, Beamon made a mark a few inches before his takeoff point on the runway, then qualified easily.

The next day was the long jump finals. The 6-foot-3, 22-year-old New Yorker dashed down the runway, hit the takeoff board perfectly, and flew close to six feet straight up in the air. When he landed in the sand pit, he hit so powerfully that he bounced back up and landed outside the pit. No one could believe it. The judges' measuring device wasn't long enough to record the jump, so they had to use a tape measure to measure the distance of Beamon's jump. When the judges recorded a measurement over 29 feet, they measured again, thinking it was impossible. Nobody had ever before jumped 29 feet! Then the official result was flashed on the electronic scoreboard: 8.90 meters. But Beamon didn't know what 8.90 meters meant in feet and inches. Finally, he was told that he had just jumped more than 29 feet. He almost fainted. Then he fell to his knees and started to cry.

Great Britain's Lynn Davies, the defending Olympic long-jump champion, was stunned. "I can't go on," he said. "We'll all look silly." Lynn then turned to Beamon and said, "You have destroyed this event."

Many people predicted that Beamon's long jump record would stand forever.

1968

Instead, the record stood for an amazing 23 years. Then, on August 30, 1991, United States jumper Mike Powell flew 29 feet, 4.5 inches at the world championships in Tokyo. Beamon was not upset that his record was broken. "Mine was a jump way before its time," he said. "It almost made it into the 21st century."

Year of the Pitcher

Pitchers were so dominant in Major League Baseball in 1968—perhaps the greatest year for pitchers in baseball history—that owners had to rewrite the rule book after the season to help swing some momentum back the batters' way.

Pitchers such as the Los Angeles Dodgers' Don Drysdale, the Detroit Tigers'

Denny McLain, and the St. Louis Cardinals' Bob Gibson overwhelmed opposing hitters. Drysdale pitched six shutouts in a row (the fifth was on June 4, the day of the California Presidential primary, and he was congratulated by Robert F. Kennedy in the speech Kennedy gave before his assassination), McLain won 31 games, and Gibson posted a miniscule earned run average of just 1.12. The entire American League batted only .230, and Carl Yastrzemski of the Boston Red Sox won the A.L. batting title with a .301 average—the lowest average ever to qualify a player for the batting crown.

The next year, the rules changed. The pitcher's mound was lowered and the strike zone was narrowed to give hitters more of a chance against increasingly better pitching. The changes worked. Beginning in 1969, baseball seemed to put an increased emphasis on offense, which eventually led to the tremendous explosion in home runs that we see today.

The most dominating pitcher of 1968 was Gibson, who was the National League's Most Valuable Player and received the Cy Young Award. Even though Gibson had pain in his right elbow, he had a 22–9 record (including 15 straight wins), with 13 shutouts and 268 strikeouts. His earned run average was the lowest ever by a pitcher who had worked at least 300 innings. His efforts were a big reason the Cardinals made World Series appearances in 1964, 1967, and 1968.

In the 1968 World Series opener in October, Gibson squared off against McLain, who went 31–6 during the regular season (he is the only pitcher since Dizzy Dean in 1934 to win 30 or more games in a

Historic Landing *Bob Beamon burrows into the sand pit at the end of the Olympic long jump after shattering the world record—and shocking even himself—by leaping more than 29 feet.*

Other Milestones of 1968

✔ In April, the Naismith Memorial Basketball Hall of Fame opened in Springfield, Massachusetts. James Naismith invented the game while a YMCA teacher in that city in 1891.

✔ At the 1968 Olympics, American Lee Evans won the 400-meter sprint in a world record time of 43.86 seconds. The record was unbeaten for 20 years, until Butch Reynolds ran 43.29 seconds. Evans also anchored the 4-by-400-meter relay team to the world record and another gold medal.

Dick Fosbury

✔ Also at the Mexico City Games, shot putter Al Oerter of the United States won his fourth gold medal. He became the first track-and-field Olympian to win his event four straight times.

✔ High jumper Dick Fosbury revolutionized his sport (and won a gold medal at the Mexico City Olympics) by performing the high jump in a new way. Fosbury would leap backward over the bar, face up, as opposed to the old "Western Roll," face-down style. His new move was called the Fosbury Flop.

---

single season). Gibson was overpowering, and the Cardinals' right-hander struck out 17 Detroit Tigers, setting a record for most strikeouts in a World Series game. The Cardinals won the game 4–0. Gibson beat McLain again in game four, but his luck ran out in the seventh game when a misjudged fly ball by Cardinal center-fielder Curt Flood led to three Tiger runs. Detroit's Mickey Lolich held on to a 4–1 victory, his third win of the Series.

Football Versus Heidi

The Oakland Raiders defeated the New York Jets 43–32 in an American Football League game in Oakland on November 17. It was an important regular-season matchup between two of the best teams in the league that season, but that's not why it deserves space here. Instead, the game had a lasting impact on televised sports after most of the country missed the exciting conclusion to accommodate *Heidi*, a children's television movie. In fact, the game is still known as the "Heidi game." When the game ran late, NBC stuck to its regular schedule and cut to the movie *Heidi*. In a thrilling finish, Oakland scored twice in nine seconds and beat the Jets, 43–32. Football fans were furious because they had missed the best part of the game. The TV networks promised never to let that happen again. Now, when football games run long, they continue covering the game.

1969

Namath Keeps Promise

Three days before Super Bowl III between the NFL's Baltimore Colts and the AFL's New York Jets was to be played in Miami, Jets quarterback Joe Namath (b.1943) approached the podium at the Miami Touchdown Club to accept an award.

"Hey, Namath, we're gonna kick your butt," a heckler bellowed. Namath, admittedly frustrated at reading all week how his team didn't even belong on the same field as the powerful Colts, got a little hot under the collar. "Wait a minute, pal, I've got news for you," he said. "We're going to win this game. I guarantee it." When the Jets stunned the Colts 16–7 January 12,

Broadway Joe

People talked about Jets quarterback Joe Namath. He excited fans by wearing fur coats and appearing in television commercials wearing women's panty hose. It didn't hurt, either, that he was a handsome 6-foot-2, black-haired star with a brash, fun-loving lifestyle. "Namath has the presence of a star," said Jets owner Sonny Werblin. "You know how a real star lights up a room when he comes in? Joe has that quality."

Namath's personal life was relentlessly publicized, and his penthouse apartment, with its famous white llama rug, was often the scene of get-togethers and parties. "A get-together," Namath once said, "is when the guys come over to eat steaks and play cards. A party is when there are girls."

While Namath's lifestyle won him the enthusiastic admiration of young fans, it raised the eyebrows of football's old guard.

Namath was the part owner of a New York nightclub called Bachelors III. In the weeks following the Super Bowl victory, much was written about Namath that tried to link him to known criminals who frequented his nightclub. When NFL commissioner Pete Rozelle ordered Namath to sell his stake in the club because of these supposed undesirable customers, Namath instead decided to retire from football. In July, after six weeks of anguish over his decision, Namath said he "just wanted to play football," ended his retirement, and agreed to sell his share of the nightclub.

Super Joe   *Quarterback Joe Namath (12) guided the Jets to a surprise championship.*

Namath's guarantee instantly became a part of pro football lore.

The NFL's Green Bay Packers had cruised to victory in the first two Super Bowls, and it seemed as if it would take years for the AFL to catch up with its older rival. And when the Colts entered Super Bowl III with a 15–1 record and a snarling defense that had shut out the Cleveland Browns 34–0 in the NFL Championship Game, the matchup didn't seem fair.

When the Jets won, though, it altered the face of pro football. The Jets' victory proved that the new league was good enough to merge with the NFL, and eased the way for three established NFL teams (the Colts, Pittsburgh Steelers, and Cleveland Browns) to move from the NFC to the AFC when the merger was complete for the 1970 season. The switch evened the conferences at 13 teams each. Each conference currently has 16 teams.

1969

Scoring Machine

Pete Maravich (1947–1988), the Louisiana State University basketball scoring machine, finished his junior season with 1,148 points, setting an NCAA single-season scoring record. The flashy 6-foot-5 sharpshooter known as "Pistol Pete" was even better in his senior season, when he scored 1,381 points for an average of 44.5 points a game—records that still stand.

Nobody in college basketball history has ever scored like Maravich. He is the all-time college leader in points scored (3,667), career scoring average (44.2), and games in which he scored 50 or more points (28, including what was then a Division I-record 69 points in 1970). He was the NCAA scoring leader and an All-America selection three consecutive seasons while at LSU, from 1968 to 1970.

Maravich averaged at least 20 points a game each season during his 10-year professional career with the Atlanta Hawks, New Orleans Jazz, and Boston Celtics. He was a two-time All-Star and, in 1976–77 with the Jazz, led the league with 31.1 points a game. He retired in 1980. Maravich died of a heart attack in 1988 while playing pickup basketball in a church gym. He was 40 years old.

Alcindor Does It Again

In the 1960s, freshmen were not eligible to compete at the varsity level in major college sports. That might be the only reason UCLA center Lew Alcindor left school following the 1968–69 college basketball season with only three national championships instead of four. Alcindor capped his spectacular career with UCLA by leading the Bruins to a 92–72 victory over Purdue University for an unprecedented third straight NCAA championship on March 22.

Alcindor scored 37 points and grabbed 20 rebounds in 36 minutes in the title game. He played on three varsity teams in college that recorded an amazing 88 wins in 90 games. UCLA went 30–0 his sophomore year, then the team went 29–1 in his junior year, and this year's squad was 29–1. The title was the fifth in six years for Bruins coach John Wooden.

New Star in the Blocks

At 7-foot-1, Lew Alcindor towered over his college basketball opponents. In the NBA, though, Wes Unseld proved that you don't have to be a 7-footer to get the job done. Although Unseld was only 6-foot-7, he was one of basketball's best centers. In his first season with the Baltimore Bullets, Unseld ranked second in the National Basketball Association with 18.2 rebounds per game and was named the league's Rookie of the Year and its Most Valuable Player. Unseld and Wilt Chamberlain are the only NBA players to receive those two honors in the same season. Candace Parker earned those dual honors in the WNBA in 2008.

Dueling Thoroughbreds

Bill Hartack (b.1932) won his record-tying fifth Kentucky Derby by riding Majestic Prince to victory by a neck over Arts and Letters on May 3. The Derby stretch duel between Majestic Prince and Arts and Letters set the stage for a rivalry that continued into the Preakness Stakes, won by Majestic Prince by a head, and the Belmont Stakes, won by Arts and Letters by five lengths. Arts and Letters' victory in the Belmont denied Majestic Prince's bid at the Triple Crown.

From 1941 to 1948, there were four Triple Crown winners, but no horse accomplished the feat again until Secretariat in 1973. Despite winning nine of 10 races and beating Arts and Letters two races to one in head-to-head competition, Majestic Prince lost out to Arts and Letters in voting for the best three-year-old of the Thoroughbred racing season and for Horse of the Year.

Déjà Vu All Over Again

Not again! For the seventh time in 11 years, the Los Angeles Lakers lost the National Basketball Association championship to the Boston Celtics. The Lakers, with three future Hall of Famers in their starting five—Wilt Chamberlain, Elgin Baylor, and Jerry West—were favored in the finals, but the Celtics came through in the clutch as usual, winning the seventh game in Los Angeles, 108–106, on May 5. Center Bill Russell, who played his farewell season, led the Celtics to their 11th title in 13 years. Russell, who also served as Boston's coach (he succeeded Red Auerbach in that capacity in 1966), averaged more than 20 rebounds per game in the playoffs.

The NBA awarded a playoff Most Valuable Player award for the first time, and West was the winner, although his team lost in the Finals. West's form on the court was picture perfect. For proof, check out the NBA logo. The player dribbling straight at you is none other than West. The NBA has used Jerry's silhouette on its logo for the past 30 years.

Indy, Italian Style

Mario Andretti (b.1940) drove his blazing red Hawk-Ford racing car to victory at the Indianapolis 500 on May 30. Upon reaching the winners' circle, Andretti was kissed on the lips by car owner

Super Mario *Mario Andretti is all smiles after taking the checkered flag at the Indianapolis 500. Andretti went on to win the Indy car season championship for 1969, too.*

1969

Andy Granatelli, the president of the STP Corporation (whose initials stand for scientifically treated petroleum, an oil additive product for automobiles).

The most versatile driver racing has ever known, Andretti won races on paved tracks, road courses, and dirt tracks in the same season four different times. The 5-foot-6, 138-pounder competed successfully in all three major types of racing: Indy car, stock car, and Formula One. He is the only driver ever to win the Daytona 500 stock car race (1967), the Formula One driving championship (1968), and the Indy car racing championship (1965, 1966, 1969, 1984)!

Stock car racing gets its name because the cars used are common brands of cars, such as Dodge, Chevrolet, and Ford. Indy cars have rear engines and open cockpits. Formula One cars are the smallest in size and are made to handle the tough curves and hills of the Grand Prix courses in Europe. Each type of car requires a special skill to drive it, which makes Andretti's achievements that much more remarkable.

Andretti grew up in Trieste, Italy, before his family came to the United States and settled in Nazareth, Pennsylvania. He began racing cars in 1961, and his 52 Indy car victories ranks second on the all-time list. He also won 12 Formula One races. Andretti retired in 1994, but the Andretti name lives on in driving circles. Mario's son, Michael (b.1962) is also an Indy car driving champion (1991) and the winningest active driver on the Indy circuit. With 42 victories, Michael trails his father by just 10 wins on the all-time list.

Racing Heats Up

Beginning in 1971, any stock-car driver that won three of NASCAR's top four races in the same season earned a cool $1 million bonus. Unfortunately, that came two years too late for auto racer Lee Roy Yarbrough of Columbia, South Carolina. He made history in 1969 by becoming the first stock-car racer to win three of NASCAR's major races in the same season. Yarbrough drove his Ford into Victory Lane at the Daytona 500 and the Southern 500, and won the World 600 in a Mercury. Yarbrough won seven races in 1969 for total earnings of $188,605.

The R.J. Reynolds Tobacco Company, makers of Winston cigarettes, sponsored NASCAR's championship series from 1971 to 2003. The Winston Cup offered a $1 million bonus to any driver who won three of NASCAR's top four events in the same season. These races included the richest (Daytona 500 in Florida), the fastest (Talladega 500 in Alabama), the longest (World 600 at Charlotte, North Carolina), and the oldest (Southern 500 at Darlington, South Carolina). No driver won all four races, and only four drivers—Yarbrough (1969), David Pearson (1976), Bill Elliott (1985), and Jeff Gordon (1997)—won three. Yarbrough was the only one of the four to miss out on collecting the $1 million bonus.

The Miracle Season

Almost all expansion teams in any professional sport struggle in their early years. But baseball's New York Mets took expansion follies to new heights—or

Tom Terrific *Pitcher Tom Seaver and the New York Mets were on top of the baseball world in 1969.*

depths—in the early 1960s. The Mets began play in 1962 in the 10-team National League and lost a record 120 of 162 games to finish last, an unfathomable 60 1/2 games out of first place. They dropped at least 109 games each of the next three seasons, too, and in their first seven years escaped the cellar only twice—both times in ninth place.

No one was prepared, then, for what came in 1969, when both the N.L. and A.L. expanded to 12 teams and divisional play began. Each league was divided into two six-team divisions, Eastern and Western. The winners of the two divisions met in a league championship series for the pennant, and the pennant winners went to the World Series.

In July, astronaut Neil Armstrong became the first person to walk on the moon. Soon after, the 1969 baseball season gave us perhaps the most improbable story in sports history. The Mets won 25 of 34 games in September to overtake the Chicago Cubs for first place in the N.L. Eastern Division, then swept the Atlanta Braves in three games to win the N.L. pennant. Then, in October, the Mets stunned the world by beating the mighty Baltimore Orioles in the World Series in five games. It was possibly the biggest upset in World Series history. It was the Mets' first winning season, and they became known as the "Miracle Mets."

No one did more to convert the New York Mets from lovable losers to the Miracle Mets than ace pitcher Tom Seaver (b.1944). "Tom Terrific" joined the Mets in 1967. At age 23, he immediately became the ace of the Mets' staff. He

1969

won 16 games in his first year for a team that won only 61, and was named the NL Rookie of the Year. Two years later, Seaver won 25 regular-season games and lifted the Mets from their ninth-place finish in 1968 to the N.L. East title. Fittingly, Seaver started and won the first postseason game in Mets' history, which was also the first National League Championship Series game. Seaver then won one World Series game, and took home the first of his three Cy Young Awards.

Texas No Turkey

The top-ranked University of Texas Longhorns traveled to Fayetteville, Arkansas, to play the second-rated University of Arkansas Razorbacks in a Southwest Conference football showdown on December 5. It was only the thirteenth time since the Associated Press' college football poll debuted in 1936 that No. 1 played No. 2—and it produced the most exciting finish of those matchups. The Longhorns rallied from a 14-point deficit in the fourth quarter to win 15–14.

Both teams entered the contest riding high: Texas had an 18-game winning streak, and Arkansas's streak was 15 in a row. Texas' Darrell Royal, in his 15th year as coach of the Longhorns, was showing off the new Wishbone offense. The Wishbone is a variation of the T-formation in which the halfbacks line up farther from the line of scrimmage than the fullback, giving the backfield the appearance of a wishbone. Royal started using the Wishbone the season before. He made the

Who Started the High Five?

The high five became popular when a national television audience saw it done by the Los Angeles Dodgers in the 1970s. The Dodgers may have raised the first high five in baseball, but they don't necessarily deserve credit for starting it.

The first Dodger high five took place on October 5, 1977, in game two of the National League playoffs. Leftfielder Dusty Baker hit a grand slam off Philadelphia Phillies pitcher Jim Lonborg, and when he returned to the dugout, he and teammate Glenn Burke raised their arms overhead and slapped hands.

"That was it—the first [baseball] high five," recalls Baker, now the manager of the Chicago Cubs. "But I didn't originate it."

The first high five probably occurred during a volleyball game played on a California beach. In fact, Kathy Gregory, women's volleyball coach at the University of California at Santa Barbara, recalls that high fives and high tens first became common in her sport as early as the late 1960s, perhaps because players were used to reaching up high and hitting their hands above the net.

"If a girl hit a ball out or made some other mistake, we just went up and high-slapped her," Gregory told *Sports Illustrated*. "You know, women give so much more support to each other than men do....For every one high five they did, we must have high-fived a million times."

Other Milestones of 1969

✔ Boston Bruins center Phil Esposito became the first NHL player to score 100 or more points in a season when he scored two goals in Boston's 4–0 victory over the Pittsburgh Penguins at Boston Garden on March 2. The NHL had at least one 100-point scorer for the next 31 years in a row.

✔ Former Canadian prime minister Lester B. Pearson was among 29,184 in attendance April 14 for the first major-league baseball game played outside the United States. The host Montreal Expos, an expansion team, beat the St. Louis Cardinals 8–7 at Jarry Park. (The Expos moved into Olympic Stadium in 1977.)

Lester B. Pearson

✔ The Alabama International Motor Speedway, now called the Talladega Superspeedway, opened. At 2.66 miles, Talladega is the world's largest motor sports oval track. The first Talladega 500 was won by Richard Brickhouse on September 14 in a Dodge at an average speed of 153.78 miles per hour. Mark Martin set a track record in his Ford in 1997, taking the checkered flag with an average speed of 188.35 mph.

✔ Steve Carlton of the St. Louis Cardinals pitched the game of his life, and lost. On September 15, Carlton struck out 19 batters (then a record), but the New York Mets' Ron Swoboda hit a pair of two-run homers in his team's 4–3 win.

switch in the backfield because he had three excellent running backs. With only one split end, the wishbone offense is designed for running instead of passing.

The 1969 Texas squad scored an average of 44 points per game during the season and, led by halfback Jim Bertelsmann, led the nation in rushing with an average of 363 yards per game. But against Arkansas, Texas was losing 14–0 after three quarters. With his team down by two touchdowns before 44,000 screaming Arkansas fans, including President Richard M. Nixon, Texas quarterback James Street went to work. First, he broke off a 42-yard touchdown run and sneaked in for a two-point conversion, cutting the deficit to 14–8. Then, on a short yardage, fourth-down play, with Arkansas expecting a run, Street went to the air and connected on a 44-yard pass that set up the go-ahead touchdown with 3:58 remaining.

Arkansas still had one last chance for a game-winning score and drove into Texas territory. But the Longhorns sealed the win with an interception at the 21-yard line.

Texas beat a tough Notre Dame squad in the Cotton Bowl on January 1 to finish the season with an 11–0 record and its second national championship of the decade (the other was in 1963). Texas went on to win 30 consecutive games with the wishbone offense before losing to Notre Dame in the Cotton Bowl at the end of the 1970 season.

RESOURCES

1960s Events and Personalities

The Encyclopedia of Sixties Cool
By Chris Strodder (New York: Penguin, 2007)
Want to know what the 1960s were like? This book is a fun overview of pop culture in the decade. It's billed as a "celebration of the grooviest people, events, and artifacts" of the decade.

Johnny U: The Life and Times of John Unitas
By Tom Callahan (New York: Crown Publishing Group, 2006)
A recent biography of the legendary NFL quarterback.

Muhammad Ali: The World's Champion
By Stephen Timblin (New York: Sterling, 2010)
A new biography of the boxing great aimed at middle-grade students.

The Official Vince Lombardi Playbook
By Phil Barber (Guilford, Connecticut: Lyons Press, 2009)
Classic plays—many of them hand-drawn—strategies, photos and recollections by and of the legendary NFL coach.

American Sports History

The Complete Book of the Olympics
By David Wallechinsky and Jaime Loucky (London: Aurum Press, 2008)
An extremely detailed look at every Winter and Summer Olympics from 1896 to the present, including complete lists of medal winners and short biographies of important American and international athletes.

The Encyclopedia of North American Sports History, Second Edition
Edited by Ralph Hickok (New York: Facts On File, 2002)
This title includes articles on the origins of all the major sports as well as capsule biographies of key figures.

Encyclopedia of Women and Sport in America
Edited by Carol Oglesby et al. (Phoenix: Oryx Press, 1998)
A large overview of not only key female personalities on and off the playing field, but a look at issues surrounding women and sports.

Encyclopedia of World Sport
Edited by David Levinson and Karen Christensen (New York: Oxford University Press, 1999)
This wide-ranging book contains short articles on an enormous variety of sports, personalities, events, and issues, most of which have some connection to American sports history. This is a great starting point for additional research.

The ESPN Baseball Encyclopedia

Edited by Gary Gillette and Pete Palmer (New York: Sterling, 2008, fifth edition)

This is the latest version of a long-running baseball record and stats books, including the career totals of every Major Leaguer. Essays in the book cover baseball history, team history, overviews of baseball in other countries, and articles about the role of women and minorities in the game.

ESPN SportsCentury

Edited by Michael McCambridge (New York: Hyperion, 1999)

Created to commemorate the 20th century in sports, this book features essays by well-known sportswriters as well as commentary by popular ESPN broadcasters. Each decade's chapter features an in-depth story about the key event of that time period.

NFL Record & Fact Book

Edited by Jon Zimmer, Randall Liu, and Matt Marini (New York: Time Inc. Home Entertainment, 2009)

An indispensable reference source for NFL fans and media personnel.

The Sporting News Chronicle of 20th Century Sports

By Ron Smith (New York: BDD/Mallard Press, 1992)

A good single-volume history of key sports events. They are presented as if written right after the event, thus giving the text a "you are there" feel.

Sports of the Times

By David Fischer and William Taafe. (New York: Times Books, 2003)

A unique format tracks the top sports events on each day of the calendar year. Find out the biggest event for every day from January 1 to December 31.

Sports History Web Sites

ESPN.com

www.sports.espn.go.com

The Web site run by the national cable sports channel contains numerous history sections within each sport. This one for baseball is the largest and includes constantly updated statistics on baseball.

Official League Web Sites

www.nfl.com
www.nba.com
www.mlb.com
www.nhl.com

Each of the major sports leagues has history sections on their official Web sites.

Official Olympics Web Site

http://www.olympic.org/uk/games/index_uk.asp

Complete history of the Olympic Games, presented by the International Olympic Committee.

The Sports Illustrated Vault

www.cnnsi.com/vault

Since its first issue in 1954, Sports Illustrated *has been a must-read for fans everywhere. You can go down memory lane in this trove of features, photos, and covers from the magazine.*

Sports Reference

www.sports-reference.com

By far the most detailed central site, including separate sections on baseball, basketball, football, hockey, and the Olympics. The sections include player stats, team histories, records from all seasons past, and much more.

INDEX